I0134667

THE AUTUMN OF THE WEST

ESSAYS

Jorge Majfud

SPARTACUS

The Autumn of the West, 2019.

Printed in the United States of America
© Translated by
© Dr. Bruce Campbell, Saint John's University, Minnesota.
© Dr. Joseph Goldstein
Edited and designed by Sandra Robert
majfud.org | jmajfud@ju.edu
Spartacus NY. editor@spartacusny.com
ISBN-13: 978-1-7332081-1-6
ISBN-10: 1-7332081-1-9
Library of Congress Cataloging-in publication Data
Name: Majfud, Jorge, author.
Title: The Autumn of the West

SPARTACUS

Most of the selected essays that comprise this book have been originally published in magazines like *UN Chronicle*, *UNESCO Courier, The Humanist* of Washington, *Monthly Review* of New York, and newspapers like *El País* of Madrid, *La República* of Montevideo, *Milenio* of Mexico, *Página 12* of Buenos Aires, and *The Huffington Post* between 1998 and 2018.

Table of Contents

I. Introduction

Tolerance is the Wine of Nations

My father was the fourth or fifth child of twelve born in Uruguay to a Lebanese immigrant couple, she being Christian and he probably too. He lived his entire childhood in misery, digging up food from the field to eat, setting his bare feet in the cow manure to relieve the frosty early morning col, fighting with other poor people for the bones that discarded by the Tacuarembó slaughterhouse.

He was a schoolboy when he was already working with his siblings mixing mortar to make bricks or planting vegetables that later he would sell in town. As one brother would come home from school, the other would meet him at the entrance of the town in order to get his shoes to wear.

Eventually, at some point in the 1950s, my father successfully made his way to the capital city to study carpentry and radiotelephony and upon returning to his town started *Fábrica de Muebles* (Furniture Factory), as he called it, in addition to starting various businesses and founding a Rotary Club and some banking cooperatives, with some success. During the day he worked in his pharmacy or looked for some lost cow in one of his fields, and at night, for 30 years, he taught classes at the technical school. His colleagues laughed at his ability to fall asleep sitting or even standing up.

"If I could go back in life, I would work less and enjoy things more," was one of the last things he told me on the phone, not out of regret but to give me a new piece of advice, which ended up being his last. Our last conversation was light-hearted because one never knows the meaning of a moment.

One day after his funeral, as I walked through the old corners of the city of my past lives, as if taking my sadness out for a walk with the secret hope of losing it at some intersection, I crossed paths with many people, too many for the moment, most of whom I did not know or was not able to recognize after so many years. One of them told me: "I had the best time of my life when I worked for your father. The man knew how to set up projects in any city and we all went together."

"I was a student of your father," another gentleman, whom I did recognize from some years back, told me. "I was a lost boy when I met him. He gave me my first job and showed me how to be part of a team. If it wasn't for him I wouldn't be who I am today nor would I have the family that I have."

My perspective, like anybody's, is not neutral. In my view he was an austere man, generous with his own family and others, even though many would think the opposite. "For some people I am a good guy," he said, "and for others I am surely a wretch. You can't be okay with both God and the devil." It was not difficult to find faults in him, not because he emphasized this in some particular human way but because it is never difficult to find faults in others. If they say there was once a perfect guy, who went around preaching democratic love even for his enemies and they crucified him anyway, what do you expect?

This was even more evident in the world of ideological passions. We always argued about politics. He always clung to his conservative principles and I always insisted on a rebuttal. Our arguments were intense but we always resolved them in a simple way: "Well, I can see now that we are not going to reach an agreement," he said, "let's go have some wine then."

Of course, someone might say that tolerance is not the wine but the opium of the people. It is no less true that its absence is the death of nations and, even worse, the frustration of each one of the concrete lives that make up that mythological abstraction.

I loved him a lot, like any good son can love a good father. But a son never loves as much as a father does. It takes a whole lifetime to come to this realization; some, even, need two lifetimes to understand it and one more to begin to accept it. So, you can go about discovering other meanings in old memories, each one more profound than the last.

For example, in several political elections, the old man listed himself on the ballot for his party. I never voted for him. I remember my first time, at the end of the 1980s, I voted for an emerging ecological party. When I arrived home I told my father that I had not voted for him. As always, he took the news with a smile and told me that I had done well.

Now that he has died, I ask myself what in the hell was the point of all my idealistic honesty on that one election day. What was the purpose of all that petty cruelty? What good was that that petty truth, that questionable honesty?

What was the point of any of it? I ask myself this while I stare at a pile of a hundred letters written in Arabic that his parents wrote and received almost a century ago. I don't know what they say. I can only suspect that they are stories of love and heartbreak, of encounters and disagreements that my father never knew about because his family also hid from him their own frustrations, just as they hid from him all the secrets of a language that they only used in the depths of their two privates lives in a small earthen house, in the middle of a field that belonged to someone else and barely provided for survival.

What was the point of it all? I ask myself again. Then I look at my son looking out the window as I liked to do while my father worked at more useful things and I realize that I know the answer. The answer, not the truth. Because duty, what should be, is one thing, and what simply is is something else. There is no doubt about one and about the other, about the truth, probably no one even knows its name.

(2012)

II. Radical Culture

What Good Is Culture?

In 2006, in Lewisburg, Tennessee, a neighborhood group protested because the public library was investing resources in the purchase of books in Spanish. Of the sixty thousand volumes, only one thousand were published in a language other than English. The annual budget, totaling thirteen thousand dollars, dedicated the sum of one hundred and thirty dollars to the purchase of books in Spanish. The buying spree, representing one percent of the budget, enraged some of the citizens of Tennessee, causing them to take the issue to the authorities, arguing that a public service, sustained through taxes charged to the U.S. populace should not promote something that might benefit illegal workers.

Thus, the new conception of culture surpasses that distant precept of the ancient library of Alexandria. That now almost completely forgotten library achieved the height of its development in second century Egypt. Its backward administrators had the custom of periodically sending investigators throughout the world in order to acquire copies of texts from the most distant cultures. Among its volumes there were copies of Greek, Persian, Indian, Hebrew and African texts. Almost all of those decade-long efforts were abruptly brought to an end, thanks to a fire caused by the enlightened ships of the emperor Julius Caesar. Nearly a thousand years later, another deliberately-set fire destroyed the similarly celebrated library of Córdoba, Spain, founded by the caliph Al-Hakam (creator of the University and of free education for poor kids), where the passion for knowledge brought together Jews, Christians, and Muslims with texts from the most diverse cultures known in the period. Also, in this period, the Spanish caliphs were in the habit of dispatching seekers throughout the world in order to expand the library's collection of foreign books. This library was also destroyed by a fanatic, al-Mansur, in the name of Islam, according to his own interpretation of the common good and superior morality.

In the past, military rulers of Latin American dictatorships (I grew up in one of them), to exacerbate honor and patriotism, tried to clean up the Spanish language, college education and culture itself from any foreign influence, starting with ideas (people in power frequently fear other's ideas, which is understandable; words are perceived as more dangerous than money and arms and, in fact, sometimes they are). For some reason they, as the Nazis and many other self-proclaimed democratic people did and do today, never realized that there is no idea, no tradition, no language, no religion, no race uncontaminated by foreigners. By definition, every human creation is historical, that is, is the result of a long evolution and, very frequently, of short and devastating involutions.

The Tennessee anecdote perhaps represents a minority in a vast and heterogeneous country (both "real Americans" and anti-Americans hate the most beautiful characteristic of this country: diversity). But it remains significant and representative of still millions of people, frequently exacerbated by some big media shows, a practice that was invented in Germany eighty years ago.

Significant and common is the idea, assumed in that anecdote, that the Spanish language is a foreign language, when any half-way educated person knows that almost one hundred years before English, it was Spanish that was spoken in what today is the United States; that Spanish has been there, in many states of the Union for five centuries; that Spanish and Latino culture are neither foreign nor an insignificant minority: more than fifty million Hispanics live in the United States and the number of Spanish-speakers in the country is roughly equivalent to the number of Spanish speakers living in Spain. For many, the "real American" (another stereotype, as most of the "real" men and women are), often depicted as a kind of cowboy, actually derives from the Mexican vaquero (originally from the Arabic tradition, like most of the traditional

West and Southwest architectural style) who left a strong mark on both legal and illegal immigrants from the eastern US. The dollar symbol, $, is derived from the Spanish Peso (PS), the common currency until late 18th century—not to mention the Spanish Empire Flag, which is in the flag of some southern U.S. states. And so on, and so forth.

If those who become nervous because of the presence of that "new culture" had the slightest historical awareness, they would neither be nervous nor consider their neighbors to be dangerous foreigners. The only thing that historically has always been dangerous is ignorance, which is why the promotion of ignorance can hardly be considered synonymous with security and progress—even by association, as with the reigning method of propaganda, which consists of associating cars with women, tomatoes with civil rights, the victory of force and wealth with proof of the truth, or a million dollars with paradise.

According to French-American Thomas Jefferson, Spanish is a crucial language to an American. He read Don Quixote in its original language and recommended the study of both Spanish and French. However, as the revolutionary British Thomas Paine once said: "nothing can reach the heart that is steeled with prejudice."

I am not so naïve as to think that today we could have intellectual politicians like the Founding Fathers, but at least it could be convenient to consider that myths, traditions, and popular history are written based on a convenient combination of memory and forgetfulness. Sometimes it helps to mitigate the pride of ignorance—and the fire as well.

(2011)

What good is literature, anyway?

I am sure that you have heard many times this loaded query: "Well, what good is literature, anyway?" almost always from a pragmatic businessman or, at worst, from a Goering of the day, one of those pseudo-demigods that are always hunched down in a corner of history, waiting for the worst moments of weakness in order to "save" the country and humankind by burning books and teaching men how to be "real" men. And, if one is a free-thinking writer during such times, one gets a beating, because nothing is worse for a domineering man with an inferiority complex than being close to somebody who writes. Because if it is true that our financial times have turned most literature into a hateful contest with the leisure industry, the collective unconscious still retains the idea that a writer is an apprentice sorcerer going around touching sore spots, saying inconvenient truths, being a naughty child at naptime. And if his/her work has some value, in fact he/she is all that. Perhaps the deeper mission of literature during the last five centuries has been precisely those things. Not to mention the ancient Greeks, now unreachable for a contemporary human spirit that, like a running dog, has finally gotten exhausted and simply hangs by its neck behind its owner's moving car.

However, literature is still there; being troublesome from the beginning, because to say its own truths it only needs a modest pen and a piece of paper. Its greatest value will continue to be the same: not to resign itself to the complacency of the people nor to the temptation of barbarism. Politics and television are for that.

Every so often a politician, a bureaucrat or a smart investor decides to strangulate the humanities with a cut in education, some culture ministry or simply downloading the full force of the market over the busy factories of prefabricated sensitivities.

Much more sincere are the gravediggers who look us in the eyes, and with bitterness or simple resentment, throw their convictions in our faces as if they were a single question: What good is literature?

Some wield this kind of philosophical question not as an analytical instrument but as a mechanical shovel, to slowly widen a tomb full of living corpses.

The gravediggers are old acquaintances. They live or pretend to live, but they are always clinging to the throne of time. Up or down, there they go repeating with voices of the dead their utilitarian superstitions about needs and progress.

How to respond about the uselessness of literature depends on what you comprehend to be useful and not on the literature itself. How useful is the epitaph, the tombstone carved, a reconciliation, sex with love, farewell, tears, laughter, coffee? How useful is football, television programs, photographs that are traded on social networks, racing horses, whiskey, diamonds, thirty pieces of Judas and the repentance?

There are very few who seriously wonder what good is football or the greed of Madoff. There are but a few people (or they have not had enough time) who question or wonder, “What good is literature?” Soccer and football are at best, naïve. They have frequently been accomplices of puppeteers and gravediggers.

Literature, if it has not been an accomplice of puppeteers, has just been literature. Its critics do not refer to the respectable business of bestsellers or of prefabricated emotions. No one has ever asked so insistently, “what good is good business?” Critics of literature, deep down, are not concerned with this type of literature. They are concerned with something else. They worry about literature.

The best Olympic athletes have shown us how much the human body may withstand. Formula One racers as well, although borrowing some tricks. The same with the astronauts who put their first steps on the moon, the shovel that builds also destroys.

The same way, the great writers throughout history have shown how far and deep human experience, (what really matters, what really exist) the vertigo of the highest and deepest ideas and emotions, can go.

For gravediggers only the shovel is useful. For the living dead too.

For others who have not forgotten their status as human beings who dare to go beyond the narrow confines of their own primitive individual experience, for the condemned who roam the mass graves but have regained the passion and dignity of human beings, for them it is literature.

Then, yes, we can say literature is good for many things. But, because we know that our inquisitors of the day are most interested in profits and benefits, we should remind them that a narrow spirit can hardly shelter a great intelligence. A great intelligence trapped within a narrow spirit sooner or later chokes. Or it becomes spiteful and vicious. But, of course, a great intelligence, spiteful and vicious, can hardly understand this. Much less, then, when it is not even a great intelligence.

(2000)

Head-Shrinking Journalism

By the nineties, yet still in the twentieth century, I used to write for five or six hours at a time on a Czech typewriter I had bought for the price of scrap. I had found it at a Sunday fair called Tristan Narvaja, in Montevideo, something like the Madrid street fair Feria del Rastro or some *marché aux Puces* in Paris. In that lonely student room that faced an alley in the Old City, I wrote and rewrote the same chapter of a novel four or five times. The hardest part was always reducing the number of words. At least, it was that part of the literary craft that consumed me the most. Nevertheless, I did it with passion, pleasure, and without any urgency, since at that time I did not write for a publication.

When I published my first novel, *Memorias de un desaparecido*, it was partly the result of the chaotic struggle between obsessions, superstitions, and personal hallucinations with the almost impossible phenomenon of communication in a phantasmagoric world, which normally is very significant for oneself but not for the rest. I am sure that if I have managed to communicate with others using or usurping the sacred art of literature, it was thanks to successive mutilations: communication of the deepest emotions only occurs in a narrow space between one's own follies and the particularities of others.

Thanks to this little novel, in a few months I met several young journalists whose friendship I retain to the present day. One day, one of them asked me to write an article on the subject of a conversation we had had, warning me that he only had space for just four thousand words. I never imagined that, for the misery of so many readers, that one would be the first article of many hundreds I have published to date. Occasionally I find that many of them have been republished in newspapers and magazines, sometimes erroneously signed by others. I usually just need to read two sentences to see if I or someone else wrote it, even when it is a fifteen-year-old article. I normally always excuse these errors but I strongly object, with some success, when I find my name on items that I never wrote. It is not good to kidnap merits or take the blame for the follies of others.

At the end of the century, you could still find short articles of four or five thousand words in nonacademic publications. Soon I could feel, beyond just understanding, the educational benefit of reducing long essays to this number, which at first seemed so greedy.

Within the first three or four years of this century, publishers had modified their typical word count from 4,000 to 2,000. I remember a major Mexican newspaper that once returned my usual weekly article because it surpassed the limit of 1,800 words. They kindly suggested that I reduce it to that number. So I did, sure that brevity is a form of kindness, and continued publishing there and in other newspapers of the continent, which apparently felt more comfortable with the new format.

A few years later, the sacred number had shrunk to 1,200, which coincided again with the standard of the entire continent, and one or two years later it reached the milestone of one thousand words.

Not long ago, one of the world's most-read media outlets asked me on four separate occasions to reduce an article to 800 words. The first time, I sent an article of a thousand words. They said I should make an effort to trim it down to 850. I sent another 900-word piece, assuming some flexibility from them. Rejected. Normally, I would have given up on sending another version, but I was very interested in publishing the article in question because its subject matter was near and dear to me. Pained, I mutilated it again to make it 850 words. Naturally, it was published.

To date, the float level of op-eds walks the 800-word limit, and dis-counting.

Now, except for the brochures and pamphlets that fill our mailboxes every day and bestsellers sold by the kilogram, this dramatic, unlimited reduction of texts in the current media is not due to a space issue, as in the times since the ancient Egyptians and Sumerians, for convent scribes, incunabula, heretics hermeneutics, the French *encyclopédistes*, and all paper periodicals from the eighteenth century to the twentieth. It is due to the new reader.

I do not intend to propose *Being and Nothingness* by Sartre as a reading model, but I do recommend it at least as an intellectual exercise. The problem is that every day we have more writing to pay attention to. Almost all are distractions; nearly all are failed stimuli. We do not have more options than before; that is patently false. We just have more distractions and, consequently, more need to interrupt everything right after we start it.

But the day of every man and woman still has twenty-four hours. The same twenty-four hours a reader of Flaubert and Dostoyevsky, Kafka and Ernesto Sabato had. Therefore, we have the same time to deal with more things and get to the bottom of them.

I am afraid that this Jivaroan head-shrinking practice that affects literature is not due to the quality of the writings, but to the shortcomings of the new reader (apart from a blind pride and self-indulgency, almost always justified with the generational excuse that prevents them from expressing any self-criticism); not due to the art of synthesis but of mutilation.

I fear that this exercise of reduction will soon become an effort to stretch an idea down to 144 characters. Possibly just 10 or 20. Probably the New Thought movement could manage quite well with a couple of emoticons. :/

(2011)

HUMANISM, THE WEST'S LAST GREAT UTOPIA

One of the characteristics of conservative thought throughout modern history has been to see the world as a collection of more or less independent, isolated, and incompatible compartments. In its discourse, this is simplified in a unique dividing line: God and the devil, us and them, the true men and the barbaric ones. In its practice, the old obsession with borders of every kind is repeated: political, geographic, social, class, gender, etc. These thick walls are raised with the successive accumulation of two parts fear and one part safety.

Translated into a postmodern language, this need for borders and shields is recycled and sold as micropolitics, which is to say, a fragmented thinking (propaganda) and a localist affirmation of social problems in opposition to a more global and structural vision of the Modern Era gone by.

These regions are mental, cultural, religious, economic and political, which is why they find themselves in conflict with humanistic principles that prescribe the recognition of diversity at the same time as an implicit equality on the deepest and most valuable level of the present chaos. On the basis of this implicit principle arose the aspiration to sovereignty of the states some centuries ago: even between two kings, there could be no submissive relationship; between two sovereigns there could only be agreements, not obedience. The wisdom of this principle was extended to the nations, taking written form in the first constitution of the United States. Recognizing common men and women as subjects of law ("We the people…") was the response to personal and class-based absolutisms, summed up in the outburst of Luis XIV, "l'Etat c'est Moi." Later, the humanist idealism of the first draft of that constitution was relativized, excluding the progressive utopia of abolishing slavery.

Conservative thought, on the other hand, traditionally has proceeded in an inverse form: if the regions are all different, then there are some that are better than others. This last observation would be acceptable for humanism if it did not contain explicitly one of the basic principles of conservative thought: our island, our bastion is always the best. Moreover: our region is the region chosen by God and, therefore, it should prevail at any price. We know it because our leaders receive in their dreams the divine word. Others, when they dream, are delirious.

Thus, the world is a permanent competition that translates into mutual threats and, finally, into war. The only option for the survival of the best, of the strongest, of the island chosen by God is to vanquish, annihilate the other. There is nothing strange in the fact that conservatives throughout the world define themselves as religious individuals and, at the same time, they are the principal defenders of weaponry, whether personal or governmental. It is, precisely, the only thing they tolerate about the State: the power to organize a great army in which to place all the honor of a nation. Health and education, in contrast, must be "personal responsibilities" and not a tax burden on the wealthiest. According to this logic, we owe our lives to the soldiers, not to the doctors, just like the workers owe their daily bread to the rich

At the same time that conservatives hate Darwin's Theory of Evolution, they are radical partisans of the law of the survival of the fittest, not applied to all species but to men and women, to countries and societies of all kinds. What is more Darwinian than the roots of corporations and capitalism?

For the suspiciously celebrated professor of Harvard, Samuel Huntington, "imperialism is the logic and necessary consequence of universalism." For us humanists, no: imperialism is just the arrogance of one region that imposes itself by force on the rest, it is the annihilation of that universality, it is the imposition of uniformity in the name of universality.

Humanist universality is something else: it is the progressive maturation of a consciousness of liberation from physical, moral and intellectual slavery, of both the oppressed and the oppressor in the final instant. And there can be no full consciousness if it is not global: one region is not liberated by oppressing the others, woman is not liberated by oppressing man, and so on. With a certain lucidity but without moral reaction, Huntington himself reminds us: "The West did not conquer the world through the superiority of its ideas, values or religion, but through its superiority in applying organized violence. Westerners tend to forget this fact, non-Westerners never forget it."

Conservative thought also differs from progressive thought because of its conception of history: if for the one history is inevitably degraded (as in the ancient religious conception or in the conception of the five metals of Hesiod) for the other it is a process of advancement or of evolution. If for one we live in the best of all possible worlds, although always threatened by changes, for the other the world is far from being the image of paradise and justice, for which reason individual happiness is not possible in the midst of others' pain.

For progressive humanism there are no healthy individuals in a sick society, just as there is no healthy society that includes sick individuals. A healthy man is not possible with a grave problem of the liver or in the heart, just like a healthy heart is not possible in a depressed or schizophrenic man. Although a rich man is defined by his difference from the poor, nobody is truly rich when surrounded by poverty.

Humanism, as we conceive of it here, is the integrative evolution of human consciousness that transcends cultural differences. The clash of civilizations, the wars stimulated by sectarian, tribal and nationalist interests can only be viewed as the defects of that geo-psychology.

Now, we should recognize that the magnificent paradox of humanism is double: 1) it consisted of a movement that in great measure arose from the Catholic religious orders of the 14th century and later discovered a secular dimension of the human creature, and in addition 2) was a movement which in principle revalorized the dimension of man as an individual in order to achieve, in the 20thcentury, the discovery of society in its fullest sense.

I refer, on this point, to the conception of the individual as opposed to individuality, to the alienation of man and woman in society. If the mystics of the 14th century focused on their self as a form of liberation, the liberation movements of the 20th century, although apparently failed, discovered that that attitude of the monastery was not moral from the moment it became selfish: one cannot be fully happy in a world filled with pain. Unless it is the happiness of the indifferent. But it is not due to some type of indifference toward another's pain that morality of any kind is defined in any part of the world. Even monasteries and the most closed communities, traditionally have been given the luxury of separation from the sinful world thanks to subsidies and quotas that originated from the sweat of the brow of sinners. The Amish in the United States, for example, who today use horses so as not to contaminate themselves with the automotive industry, are surrounded by materials that have come to them, in one form or another, through a long mechanical process and often from the exploitation of their fellow man. We ourselves, who are scandalized by the exploitation of children in the textile mills of India or on plantations in Africa and Latin America, consume, in one form or another, those products. Orthopraxy would not eliminate the injustices of the world—according to our humanist vision—but we cannot renounce or distort that conscience in order to wash away our regrets. If we no longer expect that a redemptive revolution will change reality so that the latter then changes consciences, we must still try, nonetheless, not to lose collective and global conscience in order to sustain a progressive change, authored by nations and not by a small number of enlightened people.

According to our vision, which we identify with the latest stage of humanism, the individual of conscience cannot avoid social commitment: to change society so that the latter may give birth, at each step, to a new, morally superior individual. The latest humanism evolves in this new utopian dimension and radicalizes some of the principles of the Modern Era gone by, such as the rebellion of the masses. Which is why we can formulate the dilemma: it is not a matter of left or right but of forward or backward. It is not a matter of choosing between religion or secularism. It is a matter of a tension between humanism and tribalism, between a diverse and unitary conception of humanity and another, opposed one: the fragmented and hierarchical vision whose purpose is to prevail, to impose the values of one tribe on the others and at the same time to deny any kind of evolution.

This is the root of the modern and postmodern conflict. Both The End of History and The Clash of Civilizations attempt to cover up what we understand to be the true problem: there is no dichotomy between East and West, between us and them, only between the radicalization of humanism (in its historical sense) and the conservative reaction that still holds world power, although in retreat—and thus its violence.

(2007)

Ten Lashes Against Humanism

A minor tradition in conservative thought is the definition of the dialectical adversary as mentally deficient and lacking in morality. As this never constitutes an argument, the outburst is covered up with some fragmented and repetitious reasoning, proper to the postmodern thought of political propaganda. It is no accident that in Latin America other writers repeat the US experience, with books like *Manual del perfecto idiota latinoamericano. Guide to the Perfect Latin American Idiot* (1996) or making up lists about *Los diez estúpidos más estúpidos de América Latina* (The Top Ten Stupid People in Latin America). A list that is usually headed up, with elegant indifference, by our friend, the phoenix Eduardo Galeano. They have killed him off so many times he has grown accustomed to being reborn.

As a general rule, the lists of the ten stupidest people in the United States tend to be headed up by intellectuals. The reason for this particularity was offered some time ago by a military officer of the last Argentine dictatorship (1976-1983) who complained to the television cameras about the protesters marching through the streets of Buenos Aires: "I am not so suspicious of the workers, because they are always busy with work; I am suspicious of the students because with too much free time they spend it thinking. And you know, Mr. Journalist, that too much thinking is dangerous." Which was consistent with the previous project of General Onganía (1966-1970) of expelling all the intellectuals in order to fix Argentina's problems.

Not long ago, Doug Hagin, in the image of the famous television program Dave's Top Ten, concocted his own list of The Top Ten List of Stupid Leftist Ideals. If we attempt to de-simplify the problem by removing the political label, we will see that each accusation against the so-called US leftists is, in reality, an assault on various humanist principles.

10: *Environmentalism.* According to the author, leftists do not stop at a reasonable point of conservation.

Obviously, the definition of what is reasonable or not, depends on the economic interests of the moment. Like any conservative, he holds fast to the idea that the theory of Global Warming is only a theory, like the theory of evolution: there are no proofs that God did not create the skeletons of dinosaurs and other species and strew them about, simply in order to confuse the scientists and thereby test their faith. The conservative mentality, heroically inalterable, could never imagine that the oceans might behave progressively, beyond a reasonable level.

9: *It takes a village to raise a child.* The author denies it: the problem is that leftists have always thought collectively. Since they don't believe in individualism they trust that children's education must be carried out in society.

In contrast, reactionary thought trusts more in islands, in social autism, than in suspect humanity. According to this reasoning of a medieval aristocrat, a rich man can be rich surrounded by misery, a child can become a moral man and ascend to heaven without contaminating himself with the sin of his society. Society, the masses, only serves to allow the moral man to demonstrate his compassion by donating to the needy what he has left over—and discounting it from his taxes.

8: *Children are incapable of handling stress. For which reason they cannot be corrected by their teachers with red ink or cannot confront the cruel parts of history.*

The author is correct in observing that seeing what is disagreeable as an infant prepares children for a world that is not pleasant. Nonetheless, some compassionate conservatives exaggerate a little by dressing their children in military uniforms and giving them toys that, even though they only shoot laser lights, look very much like weapons with laser lights that fire something else at similar targets (and at black people).

7: *Competition is bad.* For the author, no: the fact that some win means that others lose, but this dynamic leads us to greatness.

He does not explain whether there exists here the "reasonable limit" of which he spoke before or whether he is referring to the hated theory of evolution which establishes the survival of the strongest in the savage world. Nor does he clarify to which greatness he refers, whether it is that of the slave on the prosperous cotton plantation or the size of the plantation. He does not take into account, of course, any kind of society based on solidarity and liberated from the neurosis of competition.

6: *Health is a civil right*. Not for the author: health is part of personal responsibility.

This argument is repeated by those who deny the need for a universal health care system and, at the same time, do not propose privatizing the police, and much less the army. Nobody pays the police after calling 911, which is reasonable. If an attacker shoots us in the head, we will not pay anything for his capture, but if we are poor we will end up in bankruptcy so that a team of doctors can save our life. One deduces that, according to this logic, a thief who robs a house represents a social illness, but an epidemic is nothing more than a bunch of irresponsible individuals who do not affect the rest of society. What is never taken into account is that collective solidarity is one of the highest forms of individual responsibility.

5: *Wealth is bad.* According to the author, leftists want to penalize the success of the wealthy with taxes in order to give their wealth to the federal government so that it can be spent irresponsibly helping out those who are not so successful.

That is to say, workers owe their daily bread to the rich. Earning a living with the sweat of one's brow is a punishment handed down by those successful people who have no need to work. There is a reason why physical beauty has been historically associated with the changing but always leisurely habits of the aristocracy. There is a reason why in the happy world of Walt Disney there are no workers; happiness is buried in some treasure chest filled with gold coins. For the same reason, it is necessary to not squander tax monies on education and on health. The millions spent on armies around the world are not a concern, because they are part of the investment that States responsibly make in order to maintain the success of the wealthy and the dream of glory for the poor.

4: *There is an unbridled racism that will only be resolved with tolerance.* No: leftists see race relations through the prism of pessimism. But race is not important for most of us, just for them.

That is to say, like in the fiction of global warming, if a conservative does not think about something or someone, that something or someone does not exist. De las Casas, Lincoln and Martin Luther King fought against racism ignorantly. If the humanists would stop thinking about the world, we would be happier because others' suffering would not exist, and there would be no heartless thieves who steal from the compassionate rich.

3: *Abortion.* In order to avoid personal responsibility, leftists support the idea of murdering the unborn.

The mass murder of the already born is also part of individual responsibility, according to televised right-wing thought, even though sometimes it is called heroism and patriotism. Only when it benefits our island. If we make a mistake when suppressing a people we avoid responsibility by talking about abortion. A double moral transaction based on a double standard morality.

2: *Guns are bad.* Leftists hate guns and hate those who want to defend themselves. Leftists, in contrast, think that this defense should be done by the State. Once again, they do not want to take responsibility for themselves.

That is to say, attackers, underage gang members, students who shoot up high schools, drug traffickers and other members of the syndicate exercise their right to defend their own interests as individuals and as corporations. Nobody distrusts the State and trusts in their own responsibility more than they do. It goes without saying that armies, according to this kind of reasoning, are the main part of that responsible defense carried out by the irresponsible State.

1: *Placating evil ensures Peace.* Leftists throughout history have wanted to appease the Nazis, dictators and terrorists.

The wisdom of the author does not extend to considering that many leftists have been consciously in favor of violence, and as an example it would be sufficient to remember Ernesto Che Guevara. Even though it might represent the violence of the slave, not the violence of the master. It is true, conservatives have not appeased dictators: at least in Latin America, they have nurtured them. In the end, the latter also have always been members of the Gun Club, and in fact were subject to very good deals in the name of security. Nazis, dictators and terrorists of every kind, with that tendency toward ideological simplification, would also agree with the final bit of reasoning on the list: "leftists do not understand that sometimes violence is the only solution. Evil exists and should be eradicated." And, finally: "We will kill it [the Evil], or it will kill us, it is that simple. We will kill Evil, or Evil will kill us; the only thing simpler than this is left-wing thought."

Word of Power.

(2006)

THE IMPORTANCE OF BEING CALLED AN IDIOT

In the fall of 2006, a gentleman recommended that I read a new book about idiocy. I believe it was called *The Return of the Idiot*, *The Idiot Returns*, or something like that. I told him that I had read a similar book ten years ago, titled *Guide to the Perfect Latin American Idiot.*

"What did you think?" the man asked me narrowing his eyes, kind of scrutinizing my reaction, kind of measuring the time it took me to respond. I always take a few seconds to respond. I also like to observe the things around me, take a healthy distance, control the temptation to exercise my freedom and, kindly, go after the guy.

"What did I think? Entertaining. A famous writer who uses his fists against his colleagues as his principal dialectical weapon when he has them within reach, said that it was a book with a lot of humor, edifying… I would not say so much. *Entertaining* is sufficient. Clearly there are better books."

"Yes, that was the father of one of the authors, the Nobel Vargas Llosa."

"Mario, he is still called Mario."

"Fine, but what did you think about the book?" he insisted anxiously.

Perhaps he was not so interested in my opinion as he was in his own.

"Someone asked me the same question ten years ago", I recalled. "I thought it deserved to be a best seller."

"That's what I said. And it was, it was; in effect, it was a best seller. You realized that pretty quick, like me.

"It wasn't so difficult. In the first place, it was written by experts on the topic."

"Undoubtedly", he interrupted, with contagious enthusiasm.

"Who better to write about idiocy, am I right? Second, the authors are staunch defenders of the market, above all else. I sell, I consume, therefore I am. What other merit could they have but to turn a book into a sales success? If it were an excellent book with limited sales it would be a contradiction. I suppose that for the publisher it's also not a contradiction that they have sold so many books on the Idiot Continent, right? In the intelligent and successful countries it did not have the same reception."

For some reason the man in the red tie sensed some doubts on my part about the virtues of his favorite books. That meant, for him, a declaration of war or something of the kind. I made a friendly gesture to bid farewell, but he did not allow me to place my hand on his shoulder.

"You must be one of those who defend those idiotic ideas of which those books speak. It is incredible that a cultured and educated man like yourself could uphold those stupidities."

"Could it be that too much studying and researching cause damage?" I asked.

"No, studying doesn't do damage, of course not. The problem is that you are separated from reality, you don't know what it is to live like a construction worker or business manager, like us."

"Nonetheless, there are construction workers and business managers who think radically differently from you. Might there not be another factor? That is, for example, could it be that those who have ideas like yours are more intelligent?"

"Ah, yes, that must be..."

His euphoria had reached climax. I was going to leave him with that little vanity, but I couldn't contain myself. I thought out loud:

"It's quite strange. The most intelligent people don't need idiots like me to realize such obvious things, no?"

"Negative, sir. Negative."

After all, Mario Vargas Llosa won the Nobel Prize of Literature and left his wife for the famous Filipino model Isabel Preysler.

(2010)

THE REBELLION OF THE READERS, KEY TO OUR CENTURY

Among the most frequented sites for tourists in Europe are the Gothic cathedrals. Gothic spaces, so different from the Romanesque of centuries before, tend to impress us through the subtlety of their aesthetic, something they share with the ancient architecture of the old Arab empire. Perhaps what is most overlooked is the reason for the reliefs on the facades. Although the Bible condemns the custom of representing human figures, these abound on the stones, on the walls and on the stained glass. The reason is, more than aesthetic, symbolic and narrative.

In a culture of illiterates, orality was the mainstay of communication, of history and of social control. Although Christianity was based on the Scriptures, writing was least abundant. Just as in our current culture, social power was constructed on the basis of written culture, while the working classes had to resign themselves to listening. Books were not only rare, almost original pieces, but were jealously guarded by those who administered political power and the politics of God. Writing and reading were nearly exclusively the patrimony of the nobility; listening and obeying was the function of the masses. That is to say, the nobility was always noble because the vulgate was very vulgar. For the same reason, the masses, illiterate, went every Sunday to listen to the priest read and interpret sacred texts at his whim—the official whim—and confirm the truth of these interpretations in another kind of visual interpretation: the icons and relief sculptures that illustrated the sacred history on the walls of stone.

The oral culture of the Middle Ages begins to change in that moment we call Humanism and that is more commonly taught as the Renaissance. The demand for written texts is accelerated long before Johannes Gutenberg invented the printing press in 1450. In fact, Gutenberg did not invent the printing press, but a technique for movable type that accelerated even more this process of reproduction of texts and massification of readers. The invention was a technical response to a historical need. This is the century of the emigration of Turkish and Greek scholars to Italy, of the travel by Europeans to the Middle East without the blindness of a new crusade. Perhaps, it is also the moment in which Western and Christian culture turns toward the humanism that survives today, while Islamic culture, which had been characterized by this same humanism and by plurality of non-religious knowledge, makes an inverse, reactionary turn.

The following century, the 16th, would be the century of the Protestant Reform. Although centuries later it would become a conservative force, it birth—like the birth of all religion—arises from a rebellion against authority. In this case, against the authority of the Vatican. Luther, however, is not the first to exercise this rebellion; the humanist Catholics themselves were disillusioned and in disagreement with the arbitrariness of the Church's political power. This disagreement was justified by the corruption of the Vatican, but it is likely that the difference was rooted in a new way of perceiving an old theocratic order.

Protestantism, as the word itself says, is—was—a disobedient response to an established power. One of its particularities was the radicalization of written culture over oral culture, the independence of the reader instead of the obedient listener. Not only was the Vulgate, the Latin translation of the sacred texts, questioned; the authority of the sermon moved to the direct, or almost direct, reading of the sacred text that had been translated into vulgar languages, the languages of the people. The use of a dead language like Latin confirmed the hermetic elitism of religion (philosophy and science would abandon this usage long before). From this moment on, the oral tradition of Catholicism will continually lose strength and authority. It will have, nevertheless, several rebirths, especially in Franco's Spain. Professor of ethics José Luis Aranguren, for example, who made a number of progressive historical observations, was not free from the strong tradition that surrounded him. In *Catolicismo y protestantismo como formas de existencia* (Catholicism and Protestantism as Forms of Existence) he was explicit: "Christianity should not be a 'reader' but a 'listener' of the Word, and 'hearing it' is as much as 'living it.'" (1952)

We can understand that the culture of orality and obedience had a revival with the invention of the radio and of television. Let's remember that the radio was the principal instrument of the Nazis in Germany of the pre-war period. Film and other techniques of spectacle were also important, although in lesser measure. Almost nobody had read that mediocre little book called *Mein Campf* (its original title was *Against Lying, Stupidity and Cowardice*) but everyone participated in the media explosion that was produced with the expansion of radio. During the entire 20th century, first film and later television were the omnipresent channels of US culture. Because of them, not only was an aesthetic modeled but, through this aesthetic, an ethics and an ideology, the capitalist ideology.

In great measure, we can consider the 20th century to be a regression to the culture of the cathedrals: orality and the use of the image as means for narrating history, the present and the future. News media, more than informative, have been and continue to be formative of opinion, true pulpits—in form and in content—that describe and interpret a reality that is difficult to question. The idea of the objective camera is almost uncontestable, much like in the Middle Ages when no one or very few opposed the true existence of demons and fantastical stories represented on the stones of the cathedrals.

In a society where the governments depend on popular support, the creation and manipulation of public opinion is more important and must be more sophisticated than in a crude dictatorship. It is for this reason that television news media have become a battlefield where only one side is armed. If the main weapons in this war are the radio and television channels, their munitions are the *ideolexicons*. For example, the ideolexicon *radical*, which is encountered with a negative value, must always be applied, by association and repetition, to the opponent. What is paradoxical is that radical *thought* is condemned—all serious thought is radical—at the same time that a radical *action* is promoted against that supposed radicalism. That is to say, one stigmatizes the critics that go beyond politically correct thinking when these critics point out the violence of a radical action, such as a war, a coup d'etat, the militarization of a society, etc. In the old dictatorships of our America, for example, the custom was to persecute and assassinate every journalist, priest, activist or unionist identified as radical. To protest or throw stones was the behavior of radicals; torturing and killing in a systematic manner was the main resource of the moderates. Today, throughout the world, official discourse speaks of radicals when referring to anyone who disagrees with official ideology.

Nothing in history happens by chance, even though causes are located more in the future than in the past. It is not by accident that today we are entering into a new era of written culture that is, in great measure, the main instrument of intellectual disobedience of the nations. Two centuries ago *reading* meant a lecture or sermon from the pulpit; today it is the opposite: *to read* means an effort at interpretation, and a text is no longer only a piece of writing but any symbolic organization of reality that transmits and conceals values and meanings.

One of the principal physical platforms for that new attitude is the Internet, and its procedure consists of beginning to rewrite history at the margins of the traditional media of visual imposition. Its chaos is only apparent. Although the Internet also includes images and sounds, these are no longer products that are received but symbols that are searched for and produced in an exercise of reading.

In the measure that the economic powers that be, corporations of all kinds, lose their monopoly on the production of works of art—like film—or the production of that other genre of school desk fiction, the daily sermon where the meaning of reality is managed—the so-called *news media*—individuals and nations begin to develop a more critical awareness, which naturally is a disobedient state of mind. Perhaps in the future, we might even be speaking of the end of national empires and the inefficacy of military force. This new culture leads to a progressive inversion of social control: top-down control is converted to the more democratic control from the bottom up. The so-called democratic governments and the old-style dictatorships do not tolerate this because they are democratic or benevolent but because direct censorship of a process that is unstoppable is not convenient to them. They can only limit themselves to reacting and delaying as long as possible, by recourse to the old tool of physical violence, the downfall of their sectarian empires.

(2005)

What Is an Ideolexicon?

I have been asked several times to define what I mean by ideolexicon. I have never given the same response, but that is not due to the idea being ambiguous or undefined but quite the contrary.

Although this term is a neologism, I do not believe that at root the idea is original: everything that occurs to us others have already intuited before. It is sufficient to read those ancient Greeks in order to discover there the first indications of Darwin's theory of evolution (Empedocles), Dalton or Bohr's atoms (Leucippius or Democritus), Einstein's mass-energy equivalency (Heraclitus), modern epistemology (idem), Freud's bicephalic psyche (Plato), Derrida or Lyotard's poststructuralism (the Sophists), etc.

I suspect that the Italian Antonio Gramsci could have broadened the ideolexicon concept in the 1930s (perhaps he had already done so in his *Quaderni del carcere*, although I have not been able to find that precise moment among the more than two thousand pages of this disarticulated work). One of Gramsci's observations with regard to Marxism was the warning of a certain autonomy of the superstructure. That is, if previously it was understood that the infrastructure (the productive, economic order) determined super-structural reality (culture in general), later it was seen that the process could not only be the inverse (Max Weber) but simultaneous or dialectical (Althusser). For me, examples of the first are slavery, modern education, feminism, etc. Humanist ideals that condemned slavery existed centuries before they would be transformed into a social precept. A Marxist explanation is immediate: only when the industry of the developed countries (England and the northern United States) found an economic problem with the slavery system was the new morality (and practice) imposed. The same with universal education: the uniformity of the children's tunics, the rigorous compliance with schedules do nothing more than to adapt the future worker to the discipline of industry (or the army), the culture of standardization. For which reason today the universities and education in general have begun a reverse process of de-uniformization. Feminist demands are also ancient (and part of humanism), but they do not become a moral exigency until capitalist society and the industrialized communist societies needed new workers and, above all, new female wage workers.

Anyway, we can understand that, although these advances have not been obtained by an ethical conscience but by initial interests of the oppressors (like the universal vote for a people easily manipulable by the *caudillo* and propaganda), at any rate the road travelled "forward" is not walked backward so easily, even if those interests that made it possible were to change. Power is never absolute; it always must make concessions in order to maintain itself.

In our time, even though the use of brute force like in the times of Attila is not entirely looked down upon, it is no longer possible to lay waste to peoples and oppress other men and women without a legitimation. Much less in a global society that, though still submersed in the traditional networks of information, progressively tends to snatch from sectarian powers the *narration of its own history*. These legitimations of power may be farcical (they still trust in the fragile memory of obedient nations, or nations terrified by physical and moral violence), but their strength is the power of semantic manipulation to produce a determined reality: when a bomb is dropped from a plane and tens of innocents die, terms are used like "defense," "liberation," "collateral effects," etc. If the same bomb is placed by an individual in a market and it kills the same quantity of innocents, that act is defined as "terrorist," "barbaric," "murderous," etc. From the other side, the ideolexicons will be different: some are *imperialists*, other *rebels* or *patriots*.

In the 19th century, the Argentine D. F. Sarmiento defined José Artigas as "terrorist" (for others he was *liberator*, *rebel*), while the general Julio Argentino Roca became a military *hero*, in multiple bronze statues, because of the ethnic cleansing that his army carried out against the original owners of Patagonia ("There was no battle, it was a parade beneath the Patagonian sun and we achieved 1600 dead and another 10,000 of the rabble. It was the fate of a savage race that was already defeated," informed the venerated general Roca).

Which is to say, an ideolexicon is a word or a combination of terms (*extremist*, *radical*, *patriot*, *normal*, *democrat*, *good manners*) that has been *colonized in its semantics* with a politico-ideological purpose. This colonization generally is carried out by a hegemonic culture, but its greatest particularity is rooted in the discursive manipulation of a hegemonic political power that is disputed by resistant ideologies. The qualification of "radical" or "extremist," by possessing a negative valorization, will be an instrument of struggle: each adversary—the dominant and the marginal—will seek to associate this ideolexicon (whose *valorization* is not found to be in dispute) with those other ideolexicons whose valorization is unstable, like *progressive*, *feminist*, *homosexual*, *liberal*, *globalization*, *civilization*, etc.

In summary, an ideolexicon is a semantic weapon with a political (or socio-political) usage and at the same time it is the object of dispute of different groups in a society. When one of them is consolidated as a negative or positive value (for example, *communism*), it comes to be an instrument of colonization of other ideolexicons that are in social and historical dispute.

In its turn, each ideolexicon is composed of a positive semantic field and a negative one whose limits are defined according to the advance and retreat of the social groups in dispute (for example, *justice*, *freedom*, *equality*, etc.). That is, each group will seek to define *what is meant* and *what is not meant* by “justice,” “freedom,” at times using classical instruments like deduction and induction, but generally operating a kind of ontological declaration (A is B, B is not C) by way of association or interception of the semantic fields of two or more ideolexicons (racial integration=communism; equality + freedom=justice, etc.). When in the 1950s in the United States racial integration was in dispute, those who opposed this change demonstrated in the streets with placards: “*race mixing is communism*.” The word “communism”—like “Marxism” in Latin America—had been consolidated in its negative, demonized, values. Its meaning and valorization were not in dispute. When the soldiers of the Latin American oligarchies would murder a priest or a journalist or a unionist, whatever the case they justified themselves by adducing that the victims were Marxists, without having ever read a book by Marx and without having any more idea of what Marxism was than what they had received through strategic daily repetition.

(2005)

Virginia Tech: An Ideolexical Analysis of a Tragedy

Most of the medicines sold as pills cover a certain drug, chemical or compound with a coat that has an attractive color and a sweet taste. In Spanish, popular wisdom uses this characteristic to build a metaphor: "to swallow the pill" has a negative meaning and expresses the action of taking something with the shape or the taste of something else. In other words, it means to believe or accept a truth as an unquestionable event without being conscious of the true implications. In literary tradition this epistemological phenomenon is understood with the Trojan Horse metaphor, which is also used to name some computer viruses. An ideolexicon may be understood as a pill prescribed and imposed by a hegemonic discourse with a seductive violence. For example, the ideolexicon freedom is covered by a plethora of sweetly positive commonplaces (freedom, as a universal precept is so).

However, within this sweet and shiny covering lie the true reasons behind the actions: domination, oppression, violence against sectarian interests, etc. The sweet and brilliant cover annuls the perception of its opposites: the sour and opaque content.

The job of the critic is to break the cover, to discover, to reveal the content of the pill, of the ideolexicon. Of course, this job has bitter results, just like the center of the pill. Those who are addicted to a drug do not renounce it just because someone might discover the grave implications of their momentary comfort. In fact, they will try to resist this operation of exposition.

Let us analyze a common ideolexicon in the dominant discourse of late capitalism: personal responsibility. To start off we notice that its cover is totally sweet and shiny. Who would be capable of arguing the value of the responsibility of each individual? A possible question would be quickly annulled by a false alternative: irresponsibility. But we may start by taking the new false dilemma as the problem by observing that the adjective itself —personal—of this compound ideolexicon annuls or anesthetizes another one which is less of a commonplace and harder to appreciate by the senses: the possibility of the existence of a "social responsibility" is never mentioned. It is also never mentioned or accepted—due to a long religious tradition—that there might be "social sins."

Let us go deeper in a specific case: the tragic massacre that took place at the Virginia Tech University. Those people who—sheepishly, as always—pointed their accusing finger at the weapons culture of the United States, were criticized in the name of the personal responsibility ideolexicon. "Weapons are not what kill people," commented a friend of the rifle in a newspaper, "people are who kill people. The problem is the people, not the weapons." The pill is quite obvious, but there are once again some other problems: nobody questioned how some crazy man could kill thirty people with a stone, with a stick or even with a knife.

This logic is expressed by covering an internal contradiction in the discourse. When we talk about drugs, we are blaming the producers, not the consumers. But when we talk about weapons, we are blaming the consumers, not the producers. The reason is to be found, I believe, in the place where power is to be found. In the case of drugs, the producers are the others, not us; in the case of the weapons, the consumers are the other; we are only producing them. The hegemonic discourse never mentions that if there were no drug consumption in the wealthy countries there would be no production to satisfy that demand; if there were no illegality there would also be no drug-trafficking mafias. Or at least, their existence would be minimal, compared to what we have today. But just like the others (the producers from the poor countries) are the individuals responsible, "we" (the producers of weapons, who the administrators responsible for the law) are legitimized to produce more weapons that must be consumed by the others, to back up the law—and to break it.

If someone like the Virginia Tech killer buys a couple of guns more easily and a hundred times faster than you can buy a car and commits a massacre, all responsibility resides with the madman. We reach then a tragic paradox: a society that is armed to its teeth is entirely in the hands of crazy people who do not know how to correctly exercise their personal responsibility. In order to solve this problem, there is no turn toward social responsibility, by fighting the weapons and the economic and moral system that sustain the problem, instead more weapons are sold to responsible individuals, so that every single one of them may be more capable of performing their own "personal responsibility." Until somebody else who is exceptionally ill—in a society of saints, demons are quite frequent exceptions—appears again and commits another massacre, bigger this time, because the power of destruction of the weapons is always being improved, thanks to advanced technology and the morality of responsible individuals.

(2007)

The Terrible Innocence of Art

The idea that art exists beyond all social reality is similar to the disembodied theology that proscribes political interpretations of the death of Jesus; or to the nationalist mythologies imposed like sacred universal values; or the templars of language, who are scandalized by the ideological impurity of the language used by rebellious nations. In all three cases, the reaction against social, political and historical interpretations or deconstructions has the same objective: the social, political and historical imposition of their own ideologies. The very "death of ideologies" was one of the most terrible of ideologies since, just like the other dictatorial states of the status quo, it presumed its own purity and neutrality.

In the case of art, two examples of this ideology were translated in the idea of "art for art's sake" in Europe, and in the Modernismo of Spanish America. This latter, although it had the merit of reflecting upon and practicing a new vision with regard to the instruments of expression, soon revealed itself to be the "ivory tower" that it was. Not without paradox, its greatest representatives began by singing the praises of white princesses, non-existent in the tropics, and ended up becoming the maximal figures of politically-engaged literature of the continent: Rubén Darío, José Martí, José Enrique Rodó, etc. Decades later, none other than Alfonso Reyes would recognize that in Latin America one cannot make art from the ivory tower, as in Paris. At most, in the midst of tragic realism one can make magical realism.

Ivory towers have never been constructions *indifferent* to the rawness of a people's reality, but instead far from neutral forms of *denial* of that reality, on the artists' side, and of consolidation of its state, on the side of the dominant elites (politically dominant, that is). There are historical variations: today the ivory tower is a watchtower strategy, a secular minaret or belltower raised by the consumer market. The artist is less the king of his tower, but his labor consists in making believe that his art is pure creation, uncontaminated by the laws of the market or with hegemonic morality and politics. At the foot of the stock market tower run rivers of people, from one office to another, ascending in rapid elevators other glass towers in the name of progress, freedom, democracy and other products that spill from the communication towers. All of the towers raised with the same purpose. Because more than from contradictions—as the Marxists would assert—late capitalism is constructed from coherences, from standardized thought, etc. Capitalism is consistent with its contradictions.

The explanation of the most faithful consumers of commercial art is always the same: they seek a healthy form of entertainment that is not polluted by violence or politics, all that stuff that abounds in the news media and in the "difficult" writers. Which reminds us that there are few political parties so demagogic and populist as the imperial party of commercialism, with its eternal promises of eternal youth, full satisfaction and infinite happiness. The idea of "healthy entertainment" carries an implicit understanding that fantasy and science fiction are neutral genres, separate from the political history of the world and separate from any ideological manipulation. There are at least five reasons for this consensus: 1) this is also the thinking of the literary greats, like Jorge Luis Borges; 2) mediocre writers frequently have confused the profundity or the commitment of the writer with the political pamphlet; 3) it is justifiable to understand art from this purist perspective, because art is also a form of entertainment and pastime; 4) the idea of neutrality is part of the strength of a hegemonic culture that is anything but neutral; lastly, 5) neutrality is confused with "dominant values" and the latter with universal values.

At this point, I believe that it is very easy to distinguish at least two major types of art: 1) that which seeks to distract, to divert attention ("*divertir*" means to entertain in Spanish). That is to say, that which seeks to "escape from the world." Paradoxically, the function of this type of art is the inverse: the consumer departs from his work routine and enters into this kind of entertaining fiction in order to recuperate his energies. Once outside the oneiric lounge of the theater, outside the magical best-seller, the work of art no longer matters for more than its anecdotal value. It is the forgetting that matters: within the artwork one is able to forget the routine world; upon leaving the artwork, one is able to forget the problem presented by that work, since it is always a problem invented at the beginning (the murder) and solved at the end (the killer was the butler). This is the function of the *happy ending*. It is a *socially reproductive* function: it reproduces the productive energy and the values of the system that makes use of that individual worn out by routine. The work of art fulfills here the same function as the bordello and the author is little more than the prostitute who charges a fee for the reparative pleasure.

Different is the problematic type of art: it is not comfort that it offers to whomever enters into its territory. It is not forgetting but memory that it demands of he who leaves it. The reader, the viewer does not forget what is exhibited in that aesthetic space because the problem has not been solved. The great artwork does not solve a problem because the artwork is not the one who has created it: the exposition of the existential problem of the individual is what will lead to departure from it. Clearly in a consumerist world this type of art cannot be the ideal prototype. Paradoxically, the problematic artwork is an implosion of the author-reader, a gaze within that ought to provoke a critical awareness of one's surroundings. The entertaining artwork is the inverse: it is anesthesia that imposes a forgetting of the existential problem, replacing it with the solution of a problem created by the artwork itself.

What I mean to say is that recognizing the multiple dimensions and purposes of a work of art—which include entertainment and mere aesthetic pleasure—means also recognizing the ideological dimensions of any cultural product. That is to say, even a work of "pure imagination" is loaded with political, social, religious, economic and moral values. It would suffice to pose the example of the science fiction in Jules Verne or of the fantastical literature of Adolfo Bioy Casares. *Morel's Invention* (1940), considered by Borges to be perfect, is also the perfect expression of a writer of the Argentine upper class who could allow himself the luxury of cultivating the starkest imagination in the midst of a society convulsed by the "infamous decade" (1930-1943). A luxury and a necessity for a class that did not want to see beyond its narrow so-called "universal" circle. What could be farther from the problems of the Argentina of the moment than a lost island in the middle of the ocean, with a machine reproducing the nostalgia of an unbelievably hedonistic upper class, with an individual pursued by justice who seeks a Paradise without poverty and without workers? What could be farther from a world in the midst of the Holocaust of the Second World War?

Nevertheless, it is a great novel, which demonstrates that art, although it is not only aesthetics, is not only politics either, nor mere expression of the relations of power, nor mere morality, etc.

Freedom, perhaps, may be the main differential characteristic of art. And when this freedom does not turn its face away from the tragic reality of its people, then the characteristic turns into moral consciousness. Aesthetics is reconciled with ethics. Indifference is never neutral; only ignorance is neutral, but it proves to be an ethical and practical problem to promote ignorance in the name of some virtue.

(2005)

Puppets, Puppet Masters, and Closet Liberations

On April 5, 2010, a survey by the globally influential *Time* magazine revealed that, for its readers, Stefani Joanne Angelina Germanotta, also known as Lady Gaga, was the most influential person in the world. According to journalist Robert Paul Reyes, the singer without a doubt "perfectly captures the times."

On April 21, 2010, the investment bank Goldman Sachs reported in a triumphal tone a net profit of more than three billion dollars in the previous quarter.

On April 22, in a speech at Cooper Union, near Wall Street and with the purpose of convincing the public about his regulatory proposals for the financial system, president Barack Obama attempted to defend himself from the emerging groups on the extreme right who accuse him of being a Marxist, by asserting that he still believes in the positive power of the market. Nevertheless, "a free market was never meant to be a free license to take whatever you can get; however you can get it." Using populist discourse, according to the followers of Sarah Palin, Obama charged that "some on Wall Street forgot that behind every dollar traded or leveraged there's a family looking to buy a house, or pay for an education, open a business, save for retirement."

On Friday April 23, a Securities and Exchange Commission inspector general's memo drafted for the United States Senate and reported by ABC News, charged that during the great financial crisis of the United States which left more than eight million people jobless in 2008, several SEC inspectors who should have been controlling Wall Street were investing their labor time instead in downloading and looking at pornography. One of them achieved the record by spending eight hours a day in this activity. While only a minority of employees dedicated their work hours to pornography, more than a dozen of them were senior staffers with important responsibilities.

Meanwhile, in Gotham City, according to a United States Senate commission, the managers of the investment megabank Goldman Sachs were betting on the collapse of the real estate sector that left thousands of families homeless.

According to the *Reuters* news agency, the *New York Times* and every one of the major daily newspapers in the United States, some managers of the Goldman Sachs Group saw a chance to make some good money in the midst of the credit crisis and shortly before the mortgage collapse.

"Sounds like we will make some serious money," Donald Mullen, one of Goldman's executives, wrote in an email. Another executive, Lloyd Blankfein, faced with accusations of fraud brought by the government in a hostile reform-minded context, claimed that the company had lost money during the crisis. In September of 2008 the company received $25 billion dollars of taxpayers' money in the form of a financial bailout.

According to Democratic Senator Carl Levin, the uncovered emails show that, "in reality, Goldman made a lot of money by betting against the mortgage market." In November of 2007, according to Goldman Sachs' Chief Financial Officer David A. Viniar, the company made more than $50 million dollars in just one day by betting that mortgage securities would sink. According to the *Washington Post*, Goldman's game consisted in convincing people to invest in the real estate market at the same time that the company itself was betting in the opposite direction.

In any case the main instrument consists of promoting desire and punishing pleasure. Toward this end the social order and the hegemonic culture make use of their bankers and their religions, of their artists and their prostitutes, of their discourse about heroic and exemplary liberations from closets and dressing rooms.

Hence the importance of the populist culture and the innocence of the market for sex, of pornography conveniently called *art*, and of "authentic personal expressions" that claim to have nothing to do with politics.

Except in the perverse minds of radical critics.

Perhaps the readers of *Time* magazine are right. In a gaga society, in a planetary order dominated by superficiality and meaningless narcissism perhaps an irrelevant personality like Lady Gaga really is one of the most influential people in the world.

(2010)

INTELLECTUAL CAPITAL

In 1970 the General Motors workers' strike cut the U.S. GDP by 4 percent and is estimated to have been the reason for the poor 2 percent growth that the country experienced in the following years.

Today the decline of all U.S. automotive industries affects just one percentage point. Almost all of the GDP is in services, in the tertiary sector. In this sector, intellectual production resulting from education is growing, not to mention that today almost nothing is produced without the direct intervention of the latest computer inventions from academia, from agricultural production in exporting countries to heavy industry, mostly established in countries known as emerging or developing.

For much of the twentieth century, cities such as Pittsburgh, Pennsylvania, flourished as industrial centers. They were rich and dirty cities; such was the legacy of the Industrial Revolution. Today Pittsburgh is a clean city that lives on and is known for its universities.

In the past year, the 'research corridor' of Michigan (a consortium made up by the University of Michigan and Michigan

State University) contributed 14 billion dollars to the state from benefits generated by their inventions, patents and research. These benefits have grown over the last year and even more proportionately in a state that was the home of the big automotive industries of the twentieth century, which are in decline today.

That means that a portion of the direct benefits from one year's production of 'intellectual capital' of a university in 27th place and another one in 71st place in the national rankings, equals the total monetary capital of a country like Honduras. This intellectual production factor explains, in large part, why the economy of New York City and its metropolitan area alone is equivalent to the entire economy of India (in nominal international terms, not in domestic purchase power), a country of over a billion inhabitants and with a high economic growth rate due to its industrial production.

Today 90 percent of U.S. GDP is derived from non-manufacturing production. The monetary value of its intellectual capital is 5 trillion dollars, nearly 40 per cent of total GDP, which by itself amounts to all the items together in the dynamic Chinese economy.

If the American empire, like all empires past and future, has directly or indirectly pirated the raw materials from other countries, the fact remains that especially today the emerging countries pirate a large part of the copyrights of American inventions. Not to mention that U.S. trademark counterfeiting alone subtracts from the original products $200 billion annually, which exceeds by far the total GDP of countries like Chile.

Observing this reality, we may predict that the greatest risk for emerging countries is to allow their current development to depend on the export of raw materials; the second greatest risk is to trust too much in industrial prosperity. If the emerging countries do not invest heavily in intellectual production, they will confirm, perhaps in a decade or two, the international division of labor that sustained the great economic disparities in the 19th and 20th centuries.

Now it is fashionable to proclaim in the media around the world that America is finished, broken, three steps away from disintegration into four countries, two steps from final ruin. I get the impression that the methodology of analysis is not entirely accurate because, as revolutionary Ernesto Che Guevara criticized those who praised the effectiveness of socialist industrial production over capitalist production, it confused desire with reality. Guevara himself complained that this passion impeded any objective criticism or prevented us from seeing that the central human goal was not simply to increase the production of things.

When making predictions about the year 2025 or 2050, people used to project the present conditions onto the future scenario. This underestimates the radical innovations that even a prolonged status quo can produce along with the inevitable change on any present condition. In the early '70s, analysts and presidents like Richard Nixon himself were convinced that the emergence and ultimate success of the Soviet Union over the United States was inevitable. The '70s were years of recession and political and military defeats for the American empire.

I think that since the end of the last century we all agree that the 21st century will be a century of greater international balances. Not necessarily more stable, perhaps the opposite. It will be good for the American people and particularly for humanity for this country to stop being the arrogant power that it has been for much of its history. The U.S. has many other merits to which to dedicate itself, as history also shows: a nation of professional and amateur inventors, a nation of Nobel prizes, an excellent university system and a class of intellectuals that has opened pathways in diverse disciplines, from the humanities to the sciences.

The dramatic rise in unemployment in the U.S. is its best opportunity to accelerate this social conversion. In all international rankings, American universities occupy most of the first fifty positions. This monopoly cannot last forever, but right now that is where its principal advantage lies. Nevertheless, there is still a more crucial point.

Probably we will need to focus on "how" to develop a better understanding of "intellectual property" and its real importance in our global economy, but it is not a bad idea first to think a little about "why."

For instance, why produce so much useless stuff, why consume so much beautiful trash, such as a cheap blind that has to be replaced every six months, because it is cheap and because it does not hold up under normal use, all for the sake of "keeping the economy moving". That is, in short, why are wasting, burning and throwing away the new source of wealth? And so on and so forth.

For both questions, universities have one of the most important roles. Traditionally, the "how" is in the hands of technicians. The "why" has traditionally occupied most of the humanists. Scientists used to operate between the two of them.

Unfortunately, there are too many people without enough time to do that, too many isolated and hyperconnected individuals, too worried and too busy, thinking all the time about how to do the same thing always faster, bigger or smaller, brighter and better… Even in the academy.

(2007)

Men of the Cybernetic Caves

Every time someone complains about ideas that fall outside an arbitrary and narrow circle called "common sense" (also known in English as "horse sense"), they do so by brandishing two classic arguments: 1) the philosophers live in another world, surrounded by books and eccentric ideas and 2) we know what reality is because we live in it. But when we ask what "reality" is they automatically recite to us a list of ideas that other philosophers placed in circulation in the 19th century or during the Renaissance, when those philosophers were branded by their neighbors, if not jailed or burned alive on the holy bonfire of good manners in the name of a common sense that represented the fantasies or realities of the Middle Ages.

The Cuban poet Nicolás Guillén, perhaps in the name of what his detractors might frivolously call "populism"—as if a dominant culture were not simultaneously populist and classist by definition; what is more demagogic than the consumer market?—critiqued the idea that the poet should repeat what the people says when "misery attempts to pass itself off as sobriety" (*Tengo*, 1964). Then he recalled something that turns out to be obvious and, therefore, easy to forget: the "common man" is an abstraction if not a class formed and deformed by the communication media: film, radio, the press, etc.

Perhaps common sense is the inability of that *common man* to see the world from provinces other than his own. The first time that a common man like Colombus—common for his ideas, not for his actions—saw a Caribean, he saw the scarcity of weapons of war. In his diary he reported that the conquest of that innocent people would be easy. It is no accident that the violent enterprise of the Castilian Reconquest would be continued in the Conquest of the other side of the Atlantic in 1492, the same year the former was completed. The Cortéses, the Pizarros and other "advanced" men were unable to see in the New World anything other than their own myths through the insatiable thirst for domination of old Europe.

The old chronicles recall a certain occasion when a group of conquistadors arrived at a humble village and the indigenous people came out to meet them with a banquet they had prepared. While they were eating, one of the soldiers took out his heavy sword and split open the head of a savage who was trying to serve him fresh fruits. The comrades of the noble knight, fearing a reaction from the savages, proceeded to imitate him until they retreated from that village leaving behind several hundred indians cut to pieces. After a brief investigation, the same conquistadors reported that the event had been justified given that a welcome such as the one they had witnessed could only be a trick. In this way they inaugurated—at least for the chronicles or as slander—the first preemptive action on behalf of civilization. The popular idea that "when the charity is great even the saint is suspicious," makes heaven complicit in that miserable human condition.

In the same way, both science fiction and the plundering of resources through the colonization of new planets are nothing more than the expression of the same aggressive mentality that cannot resolve the conflicts it provokes at each step because it is already undertaking the expansion of its own convictions in the name of its own mental frontiers. The conquistadors (of any race, of any culture) can neither comprehend nor accept that supposedly more primitive beings (native Americans) as well as more evolved beings (possible extraterrestrials) might be capable of something more than a close-minded military conduct, aggressively exploitative of the barbarians who don't speak our language.

That is to say, mass consumer science fiction—that innocent artistic expression, made popular by the disinterested market—is the expression of the most primitive side of humanity. The basic scheme consists of dominating or being dominated, killing or being exterminated, like our ancestors, the Cro-Magnons, exterminated the big-headed Neanderthals—who later became the mythological ogres of the European forests—thirty thousand years ago. This genre is understandable especially in the Cold War, but it is as old as our culture's thirst for colonization. It is not surprising, therefore, that the extraterrestrials, supposedly more evolved than us, would be out there playing hide and seek. It is quite probable, besides, that they know the case of the Nazarene who took the precaution of using metaphors to preach brotherly and universal love and was crucified anyway.

Presently, while conflicts and wars ravage the whole world, while the environment is in its most critical state, scientists are charged with finding life and water on other planets. NASA plans to use greenhouse gases—like carbon dioxide or methane—to raise the temperature of Mars, melting the frozen water at its poles and forming rivers and oceans. With this method—already tested on our own planet—we will stop buying bottled water from Switzerland or from Singapore in order to import it from Mars, at a slightly higher price.

We are not able to communicate with one another, we are not able to adequately conserve the most beautiful planet in the galactic neighborhood, and we will manage to colonize dead planets, discover water and encounter other beings who probably do not want to be found by intergalactic beasts like us.

Nor is it by accident that the objective of video games is almost always the annihilation of the adversary. Playing at killing is the common theme of these electronic caves filled with Cro-Magnon men and women. If indeed we could imagine a positive side to this, like the possibility that the exercise of playing at killing might substitute for the real practice, there still remains the question of whether violence is an invariable human constant (psychoanalytic version) or can be increased or decreased through a precise culture, through a psychological and spiritual evolution on the part of humanity. I believe that both are surviving hypotheses, but the second one is the only active hope, which is to say, an ideology that promotes an evolution of the conscience and not resignation in the face of what is. If ethical evolution does not exist, at least it is a convenient lie that prevents our cynical involution. The Romans also used to express their passions by watching two gladiators kill each other in the arena; some Spaniards discharge the same passion by watching the torture and murder of a beast (I am referring to the bull). Perhaps the first replaced the imperial monstrosity with soccer; the second are in the process of doing so. A few weeks ago, a group of Spaniards marched through the streets carrying slogans like "Torture is not culture." Protest is a valiant resistance to barbarism disguised as tradition. We are better off not observing that as history shows, in reality, torture is a culture with a millenarian tradition. A culture refined to the limits of barbarism and sustained by the cowardly refinement of hypocrisy.

Bertrand Russell used to say that the madness of the stadiums had sublimated the madness of war. Sometimes it is the other way around, but this is almost always true. It is not less true, of course, that the culture of violence carries with it two hidden purposes: 1) with the supposedly violent libido sublimated in sports, films and video games, the greater violence of social injustices (injustice, from a humanist and Enlightenment point of view) remain unchallenged by the exhausted and self-satisfied masses; 2) it is a form of anesthesia, of moral habit-forming, in the periodic return of the brute, prehistoric violence of the electronic wars where one neither kills nor murders but suppresses, eliminates. This cybernetic primitivism seduces by its appearance of progress, of future, of spectacle, of technological exploits. Human ignorance is camouflaged in intelligence. Poor intelligence. But it continues to be ignorance, although more criminal than the simple ignorance of the cave-dweller who split open his neighbor's head in order to avenge a theft or an offense. Modern wars, like the genre of science fiction, are more direct expressions of a race of cave-dwellers that has multiplied dangerously its power to split open its neighbor's head but has not committed itself to the courageous enterprise of universal conscience. Instead, it defends itself against this utopia by taking recourse to its only dialectical weapon: mockery and insult.

(2006)

Power and the Intellectuals

A student once asked me: "If Latin America has always had so many good writers, why is it so poor?" The answer is multiple. First one would have to problematize a little something that seems obvious: what do we mean when we talk about poverty? What do we mean when we talk about success? I am certain that the concept assumed in both cases is the same one understood by Donald Duck and his uncle. As Ariel Dorfman observed, for the Disney characters there are only two possible forms of success: money and fame. The Disney characters neither work nor love: they conquer—if they are male—or seduce—if they are female. Which is why we never encounter among them workers or fathers or mothers.

Now, on the other hand we have to answer a rhetorical question: "And when in Latin America have the structures of power, the governments and private enterprises, ever paid any attention to the intellectuals?" The answer is again multiple. Yes, in the 19th century there were intellectual presidents, when they weren't military men. In the following century the former became scarce and the latter abundant. Although I believe it would be better to listen a little to someone who has dedicated their life to study instead of listening to so many opinions about politics, economics and culture from soccer players and movie stars, I don't believe we intellectuals should have a central voice in society or in the decisions about its future. It is curious that in these times the intellectuals don't play soccer or displace the actors from the theater stage, and don't take work from the politicians, and yet any sports figure, star of film or of "the real world" repeatedly exercises their right to publicly express their thoughts even though they might not be thoughts so much as spontaneous vibrations of the moment. An old man who has spent his life researching birds is a failure; but if Madonna or Maradona has an opinion about ornithology they are listened to and discussed on a mass scale.

In the 20th century intellectuals were systematically expelled or demoted by the power structures. According to César Milstein, when military leaders in Argentina took control of civilian power in the 1960s, they declared that our countries would be put in order as soon as all the intellectuals who were meddling in the region were expelled. In Brazil, the educator Paulo Freire was kicked out of the country for being ignorant, according to the organizers of the *coup d' etat* of the moment. To cite just two of our many cases.

But this contempt that arises from a power installed in the social institutions and from the inferiority complex of its actors, is not a property of "underdeveloped" countries. In the United States they don't listen to their intellectuals either. In fact, it is always the critical intellectuals, writers or artists who head the top-ten lists of the most stupid of the stupid in the country. Intellectuals are stupid, and those who make these lists, who are they? The same as always: prideful men and women with "common sense," as if this distorted claim to realism were not heavily laden with fantasies and ideologies at the service of the status quo. "Common sense" is what the common men and women had who asserted that the Earth was flat like a table; Calvin was a man of "common sense" who ordered that Miguel de Servet be burned alive, after he tired of arguing about theology via correspondence with his adversary. It was men of "common sense" who obligated Galileo Galilei to retract his claims and shut his stupid mouth, as were those others who mocked the pretensions of a carpenter named Jesus of Nazareth.

A character from the novel *Incident in Antares*, by Érico Veríssimo, reflected: "During the Hitler era the German humanists emigrated. As a result, the technocrats were given free reign." And later: "When president Truman and the generals of the Pentagon met, under the greatest secrecy, to decide whether or not to drop the first atomic bomb over a Japanese city… do you think they invited to that meeting a humanist, artist, scientist, writer or priest?"

(2005)

Are We Really Indebted to Capitalism for Modernity?

One of the most often repeated and least questioned assertions made by the apologists of capitalism is the one that claims that capitalism is the economic system that has created the most wealth and progress in history. We are indebted to capitalism for the Internet, airplanes, YouTube, the computers we write with, and every medical advance and all the social and individual liberties we enjoy today.

Capitalism is neither the most nor the least criminal of economic systems that have existed, but this account is, in addition to being arrogant, a hijacking of history by ignorance.

In absolute terms, capitalism is the period (not the system) that has produced the greatest wealth in history. This truth would be sufficient if we did not consider that it is as deceptive as when, in the 1990s, a Uruguayan official made much of the fact that under his administration more mobile phones had been sold than in the entire previous history of the country.

The arrival of man on the moon was not a direct consequence of capitalism. For starters, neither public nor private universities are, fundamentally, capitalist enterprises (with the exception of a few cases, as with the fiasco of Trump University). Nor was NASA ever a private enterprise, but a state agency and, moreover, was developed thanks to the prior contracting of more than a thousand German engineers, among them Wernher von Braun, who had experimented with and perfected rocket technology in Hitler's laboratories, who in turn had invested a fortune in the effort (admittedly, with economic and moral support from large U.S. corporations). Everything, money and planning, was provided by the government. The Soviet Union, mostly under the command of the dictator Stalin, won the space race by putting into orbit, for the first time in history, the first satellite, the first dog and even the first man – 12 years before Apollo 11 and barely 40 years after the revolution that turned a backward and rural country, like Russia, into a military and industrial power in the space of a few decades. None of that can be understood as capitalism.

Obviously, the Soviet system was responsible for many moral failings. For crimes. But moral deficiencies are not what distinguished bureaucratic communism from capitalism. Capitalism is only associated with democracies and human rights according to a sweeping and oft-repeated narrative (theorized by the Friedmans of the world and put into practice by the Pinochets), but history shows that capitalism can co-habit perfectly with a liberal democracy; with genocidal Latin American dictatorships operating on the pretext of a war against communism;

with communist governments like China and Vietnam; with racist systems like South African apartheid; with empires set on the destruction of democracies and millions of inhabitants of Asia, Africa, and Latin America, as was the case with England, Belgium, the United States, France, etc. in the 19th and 20th centuries.

Like setting foot on the moon, the creation of the Internet and computers, despite being attributed to capitalism, were basically (and, in some respects, exclusively) projects carried out by governments, not capitalist enterprises like Apple or Microsoft. None of the scientists who worked on those revolutionary technological programs did so as businessmen or in order to get rich. In fact, many of them were ideologically anti-capitalist, like Einstein, among others. Most of them were salaried professors, not the entrepreneurs so venerated at present.

To this reality one must add other facts and a basic idea: none of this arose from scratch in the 19th or 20th centuries. Atomic bombs and energy are the immediate and direct offspring of the imaginative speculations and experiments of Albert Einstein, followed by other salaried geniuses. The arrival of man on the moon would have been impossible without basic concepts like Newton's third law. Neither Einstein nor Newton would have developed their marvelously superior mathematics (none of it owing to capitalism) without a plethora of mathematical discoveries introduced by other cultures centuries before. Can anyone imagine infinitesimal calculus without the concept of zero, without the

Arabic numeral system and without algebra (al-jabr), to name just a few?

The algorithms used by computers and Internet systems were not created by a capitalist or during any capitalist period but centuries ago. Conceptually they were developed in Baghdad, the capital city of the sciences, by a 9th century Muslim mathematician of Persian origin whose name, Al-Juarismi, is legible in the computational term. According to Oriana Fallaci, that culture gave nothing to the sciences (ironically, capitalism is born in the Muslim world and the Christian world develops it).

Neither the Phoenician alphabet, nor commerce, nor republics, nor democracies originated in the capitalist period, but dozens of centuries prior. Not even the printing press in its different German and Chinese versions, an invention more revolutionary than Google, was a result of capitalism. Not gunpowder, not money, not checks, not freedom of expression.

Although Marx and Edison may have been a consequence of capitalism, no great scientific revolution of the Renaissance and the Modern Era (Averroes, Copernicus, Kepler, Galileo, Pascal, Newton, Einstein, Turing, Hawking) was due to capitalism.

Not to mention more practical discoveries, like the lever, the screw, or Archimedes' hydrostatics, dating to 2300 years ago. Or the 9th century compass, one of the discoveries of greatest consequence in human history, by far more significant than any smart phone. Or the wheel, which began to be used in the East some six thousand years ago and has still not fallen out of style.

Clearly, a number of centuries passed between the invention of the wheel and the invention of the compass. But the much vaunted "dizzying progress" of the capitalist period is nothing new. Except for periods of catastrophe like the Black Plague of the 14th century, humanity has long been accelerating the appearance of new technologies and of resources available for a growing portion of the population, as for example with the various agricultural revolutions. One needn't be a genius to recognize that that acceleration results from cumulative knowledge and intellectual freedom.

In Europe, money and capitalism meant social progress in the face of the static feudal order of the Middle Ages. But they soon became the engine of colonial genocides and then of a new form of feudalism, that of the 21st century, with a financial aristocracy (a handful of families acquire most of the wealth in countries both rich and poor), with political dukes and counts, and with disempowered vassals and villagers.

Capitalism capitalized on (and capitalists hijacked) centuries of social, scientific, and technological progress. For this reason, and due to be the dominant global system, it was capable of producing more wealth than earlier systems.

Capitalism is not the system of every country in the world. It is the hegemonic system of the world. Its problems can be mitigated, its myths can be dismantled, but it cannot be eliminated until it enters into crisis or decline like feudalism. Until it is replaced by another system. That is, if the planet and humanity survive. Because capitalism is also the only system that has placed the human species on the edge of global catastrophe.

(2017)

THE REAL WALLS OF AMERICAN DEMOCRACY

The walls of American democracy are of two genders: one is cultural and the other structural. Both, with an old objective: to maintain power in the hands of a minority that is represented as the majority.

Let's look at the cultural wall, first, but let's start with its positive side. The so-called Founding Fathers were an elite of intellectuals, a reflection of the new and radical European ideas that found a space in the new continent that they did not have in the old, in the same way, that Christianity did in Europe, not in Jewish Palestine. A territory less coveted by the empires of the moment and less harassed by the millenarian tradition of fossilized ideas. Thomas Jefferson had become a French citizen before becoming president of the United States, and everyone else had, in some way, a deep admiration for the philosophers of the Enlightenment. Jefferson's ideas, like that of the other founders, did not tune in much with the rest of the population, to the extent that his books were banned in many libraries under the exaggerated accusation of being an atheist. The idea of creating a thick wall to separate politics from religion was too radical.

However, this foundational elite shared with the rest the misfortune of racism and double standards. The genius of Benjamin Franklin did not want immigration that was not white and Anglo-Saxon. The sage of Thomas Jefferson not only abused a minor who became a mother several times but also never released her for being a mulatto. The beautiful slave girl, Sally Hemings, was the illegitimate daughter of her father-in-law with another slave. For not entering the long and persistent history of racist laws ranging from the idea of black inhumanity to the contempt of Latin Americans for their condition of hybridity, such as mules (mulatto), something that, according to journalists and congressmen of the 19th century, did not please God. The repulsion for the Chinese, for the Irish (before they became assimilated whites), for the Indians and the Mexicans completed the map of contempt and dispossession to all that was not Anglo-Saxon and Protestant. The beautiful phrase "We the people" assumed that with that "the people" did refer neither to the blacks, nor to the Indians, nor to anyone who did not belong to the "race" of the founders. However, Jefferson was right when he said that "the land belongs to the living, not the dead."

The Founding Fathers (and the leaders who followed them) are often excused because they were "men of their time." You cannot judge someone who lived two hundred years ago with today's values. However, a few years after Jefferson left the government in the United States, a rebel military named Jose Artigas, who was against military abuse in the government and in favor of a more direct democracy, took control of the League of Free Peoples (what is now Uruguay and part of Argentina) distributed land to whites, Indians, and blacks under the slogan "the most unhappy will be the most privileged." A truly Christian principle and attitude of a non-religious man.

Nor is it true that the United States never had a dictatorship. In fact, its laws took a century, until after the Civil War, to recognize that someone could be a US citizen regardless of the color of their skin, but then continued to filter, also by law, immigrants who were not white enough.

Currently, even the whitest whites have become blacks. But they do not know it and that is why they hate blacks and browns. They feel they are the new blacks, but they do not recognize it, and, for that reason, they need to despise the rest to confirm their former status as white, that is, privileged.

Meanwhile, the American democracy continues to be kidnapped by the 0.1 percent of its population, by the billionaires who finance the political campaigns, dine with the winners, and send scribes to sit on the committees that write the laws that legislators later approve, whose majority are millionaires.

Now let's look at the structural walls of hegemonic democracy. These problems are also rooted in racism, and social elitism masked in an opposite discourse.

Let's see this logic referring to the old obsession of ethnic bubbles. The Latino population is extremely underrepresented because, like other minorities such as African-American and Asian, they live in large cities and these are in the most populous states such as California, Texas, Florida, New York and Illinois. Of these states, only Texas is a state with a substantial conservative majority. Florida is a swing state, and the others are traditional progressive bastions (liberals, in the American language). However, even though California has a population of 40 million, it only has two senators. The same amount as New York, another state with 20 million. The same number of senators has each of the fifty states, such as Alaska, a state whose population does not reach 800 thousand inhabitants, or a collection of central states such as the two Dakotas, Nebraska, etc. with about a million inhabitants each (Wyoming barely reaches half a million), and each has two senators. Which means that a farmer's vote in any of that dozen conservative and depopulated states is worth 30 to 40 times more than the vote of an American living in the populated states of California, Texas, Florida, New York or Illinois.

Of course, this system of election of senators is not unique in the world, but in the United States the population and political imbalance in favor of rural conservatives, since the nineteenth century, is remarkable and consistent.

As if that were not enough, we must consider that its system of presidential elections not only denies Puerto Rico, with almost four million inhabitants (more than several central states together), the possibility of electing president, but also, the current electoral system, an inheritance of the slave system that favored the southern states with a small white population ("the people"), which still makes possible for a president to be elected having received three million votes less than the loser.

Thanks to this system (electors reproduce not only the number of representatives but also senators), more populated states such as California, Texas, Illinois or New York (which subsidize more impoverished states) need twice or more votes than the unpopulated central states to reach an elector. Another reason to understand why minorities, that added are not, are not treated with the electoral justice that a true democracy must guarantee: a citizen, a vote.

Not by chance the population, despite the old media manipulation, usually have very different opinions to their governments.

Which hardly matters in this democracy.

(2017)

III. Propaganda and Popular Culture

Where Does the Voice of the People Come From?

In memory of Edward Bernays,
artist of public manipulation

If naïve is not the opposite of genius, it is also not its substitute. This is the origin of fables and parables. Or of sophisms like: "I can resist anything, except temptation" (attributed to Oscar Wilde); "a communist is someone who has read Marx; an anti-communist is someone who has understood him" (Ronald Reagan); or Groucho Marx's smartest bits. The sophism is a miniscule piece of naivety that frequently stands in for or pretends to cover up the absence of a more complex thought.

Lincoln's hopeful and popular statement, "you can fool all the people some of the time, and some of the people all the time, but not all the people all the time," is similar to Churchill's, "never before have so many owed so much to so few." Perhaps phonetic geometry ("…all the people some of the time, and some of the people all the time, but not all the people all the time") conspires against historical truth. It depends on the meaning of "some of the time" and "some of the people." For despots and dictators perhaps, a couple of decades might be "so few" but to those who must suffer them a half an hour might be "so much time."

For centuries, the idea that the Sun revolved around the Earth was unanimous. Ptolemy's old system—pretty new if we consider that other Greeks understood that in reality the Earth moved around the Sun—was the "vox populi" on cosmology. The calculations that took Ptolemy's model into account were able to predict eclipses. That cosmological model was overturned, bit by bit, beginning with the Renaissance. Today heliocentrism is the "vox populi." It at least sounds ridiculous to say that in reality the Sun revolves around the Earth. Nevertheless, this reality is undeniable. Even a blind man can see it. From the point of view of an earthling, what revolves is the Sun, not the Earth. And if we consider the first Einsteinian principle which holds that there is no privileged point of view nor solitary system of observation in the Universe, there is no reason to deny that the Sun revolves around the Earth. The heliocentric idea is only valid for a (imaginary) point of view outside the solar System, a simpler and more aesthetically developed point of view.

One of the first written mentions of *vox populi, vox Dei* is made by Flaccus Albinus Alcuinus more than a thousand years ago, precisely in order to refute it: *...tumultuositas vulgi semper insaniae proxima sit* ("...the good sense of the common people is more like madness"). Its pagan and perhaps demagogic roots authorize the people in the name of God but/and are used by a whole range of atheists or anti-clericals. On the other hand, the bureaucracy that has been invented for God in order to assist him in administering his Creation, has practiced historically the opposite slogan: "the power of the king originates from God." At least from Tutankhamen through to the *generalísimos* and (not) very Catholic Franco, Videla, Pinochet and the U.S. neo-conservatives. Nor has the Vatican ever taken recourse to the "vox populi" in order to elect the "vox Dei." How could God have given us intelligence and then demanded from us the conduct of a flock of sheep?

Since the times in which feudal and theocratic propaganda reined and in the times of the absolutist monarchs, the "vox populi" was a creation of (1) pulpits and school desks and of (2) popular stories about kings and princesses. Not very different from (2) are the latest soap operas and the magazines about the Rich & Famous where the elegant miseries of the dominant classes are placed on exhibit for the moral consumption of the people. Different from (1), although not by much, the "vox populi" is formed today on the political stage and in the dominant *mass media*.

Not much different from that first black-and-white Nixon-Kennedy debate. Does the candidate exist who dares to defy the sacred "public opinion"? Yes, only the one who knows that he has no serious likelihood of winning and is not afraid to stick his finger in the wound. But politicians with a chance cannot afford the luxury of making that "vox populi" uncomfortable, for which reason they tend to accommodate themselves to the center—the ideological space created by the media—in the name of pragmatism. If the ultimate goal is angling for votes, does anyone dare to say something that he knows, beforehand, will not be well received by the voting masses? Candidates do not debate; they compete in seduction, as if they were "singing for a dream."

Now, does all this mean that the people have the authority to impose a behavior on their own candidates? Does it mean that the people have power? In order to respond we must consider whether that public opinion is not frequently created, or at least influenced by the large *communication media*—a title self-evidently false and at times demagogic—just like in the Middle Ages it was created and influenced from the pulpit and communication was reduced to the sermon and the message was, as today, fear.

Obviously, I am not going to defend freedom of the press in Cuba. But on the other hand the repeated freedom of the press of the self-proclaimed "free world" does not shine under close inspection. I am not referring only to the democratic self-censorship of those who fear losing their jobs, or to the unemployed politicians who must disguise their ideas in order to convince a potential employer. If in the "unfree" countries the press is controlled by the State, who controls the means (or media) and the ends in the free world? The people? Someone who does not belong to the select family of the large media that exercise "world coverage," who can say what kind of news, what kind of ideas should dominate the air, the land and the seas like our daily bread? When it is said that ours is a free press because it is governed by the free market, is one arguing for or against the freedom of the press and of the people? Who decides which news and which truths should be repeated 24 hours a day by CNN, Fox or Telemundo? Why is it that Paris Hilton crying over a two-week jail stay—and then selling the story of her crime and of her "moral conversion"—is front page news but thousands of dead as a result of avoidable injustices are an item alongside the weather prediction?

In order to complete the (self)censorship in our culture, each time that someone dares to examine things closely or scribble out a few questions, they are accused of preferring the times of Stalinism or some corner of Asia where theocracy reigns at its whimsy. This is, also, part of a well-known ideological terrorism about which we must be intellectually alert and resistant.

History demonstrates that big changes have been driven, foreseen and provoked by minorities attentive to the majority. Almost as a rule, national peoples have been more conservative, perhaps owing to the historical structures that have imposed on them a leaden obedience. The idea that "the people are never wrong" is very similar to the demagoguery of "the client is always right," even though it is written with the other hand. In the best (humanistic) sense, the phrase "vox populi, vox Dei" can refer not to the idea that the people necessarily are right, but to the idea that the people is its own truth. That is to say, every form of social organization has the people as subject and object. Except in a theocracy, where this rationality is a god who regrets having conferred free will on his little creatures. Except in the most orthodox mercantilism, where the end is material progress and the means to the end human flesh and blood.

(2004)

The Intra-national Colonization of Patriotisms

Once, in a high school class, we asked the teacher why she never talked about Juan Carlos Onetti. The answer was blunt: that gentleman had received everything from Uruguay (education, fame) and "he had left" for Spain to speak ill of his own country. That is, an entire country was identified with a government and an ideology, excluding and demoralizing everything else.

Implicitly, it is assumed that there exists a unique—true, honorable—form for the nation and of being Uruguayan (Chinese, Argentine, North American, French). If one is against that particular idea of country, of fatherland (patria), then one is anti-patriotic, one is a traitor.

A fundamental requirement for the construction of a tradition is memory. But never *all* memory, because there is no tradition without forgetting. Forgetting—always more vast—is indispensable for the adequation of a determined memory to the present-day powers that need to legitimate themselves through a tradition. If we assume that national symbols and myths are not imposed by God, we are left with no other remedy than to suspect earthly powers. Which is to say, a tradition is not *simple and innocent memory* but *convenient memory*. The latter tends to be crystalized in symbols and sacred cows, and there is nothing less objective than symbols and cows.

In the Spain of Isabella and Ferdinand, exclusion was the basis for a previously non-existent fatherland. The Iberian Peninsula was, at the time, the most culturally diverse corner of Europe and comprised of as many countries as the rest of Europe. Being Spanish became for many, after the Reconquest, an exercise in purification: one sole language, one sole religion, one sole race. Almost five hundred years later, Francisco Franco imposed the same idea of nation based at least on the first two categories of purity. Camilo José Cela recognized it thusly: "Not one single Spaniard is free to see Jewish or Moorish blood run through his veins" *(A vueltas con España*, 1973); like they say, "nobody is perfect." For centuries the intellectuals sought out, obsessively, the "Spanish character," as if the absence of a concrete character ran the risk of losing the country. Américo Castro in *Los españoles...* (1959) observed: "one will not find anything similar to the Spanish fantasy of imagining Spaniards before they existed." He then criticized the patriotic writings that praised what was Spanish about Luis Vives, who, even abroad "never forgot Valencia": he could not forget Valencia because his family, of Jewish origin, had been persecuted and both his parents burned by the Inquisition. The celebrated priest Manuel García Morente believed that "for the Spanish there is no difference, there is no duality between fatherland and religion" (*Idea de la hispanidad*, 1947); "there exists no dualism between Caesar and God." "Spain is made of Christian faith and Iberian blood." "In Spain, Catholic religion constitutes the purpose of a nationality…" The ultraconservative taste for essences led him to repeated tautologies of this kind: "the patriotic duty" is to be "faithful to the essence of the fatherland." Another Spaniard, Julio Caro Baroja (*El mito del carácter nacional*, 1970), questioned these functional ideas of power: "I consider that everything that speaks of "national character" is a mystical activity." "National characters are meant to be established as collective and hereditary. Thus, at times, one recurs to expressions like 'bad Spaniard,' 'renegade son,' traitor to the 'legacy of the fathers' in order to attack an enemy."

This strategy of forgetting and exclusion is universal. We Chileans, Argentines and Uruguayans constructed a tradition to the measure of our own euro-centric and not infrequently racist and genocidal prejudices. The authors of various ethnic cleansings (Roca, Rivera) are honored even today in the schools and in the names of streets and cities. Indigenous people were not only exploited and exterminated; we also ended up whitewashing the memory of the indomitable savages. Another Spaniard, Américo Castro, reminds us: "When the people are more believers than thinkers […] it becomes unpleasant to doubt."

Thus, *The* fatherland is turned into an idea of nation that tends to exclude all other ideas of nation. For this reason it usually becomes a weapon of negative domination based on the positive sentiments of belonging and familiarity. In order to consolidate that arbitrariness of traditional power, other semantic instruments are made use of. Like *honor*, for example.

Honor is the symbolic tribute that a society imposes, by way of ideological and moral violence, on those individuals who must exercise physical violence in order to defend the sectarian interests of those others who will never risk their own life to do so. For this reason, a composite and contradictory ideolexicon like "the honor of weapons" has survived for centuries. There exists no other way to predispose an individual to death for reasons he is in no position to understand or, if he understands them, he is in no position to accept as his own reasons. If it is a matter of a soldier (the most common case) the salary will never be sufficient reason to die. It is necessary to cultivate a motivation beyond death. In the case of the religious martyr, this function is fulfilled by Paradise; in the case of a secular society that organizes an army through a secular State, there is no alternative but the compensation of an exemplary death: *honor*, *fulfillment of one's duty*, *love of country*, etc. All ideolexicons based on positive, unquestionable meanings.

One honors individuals (paradoxically anonymously) because one cannot honor the war that produces seas of nameless dead, nor can one honor the financial and political reasons, the sectarian interests in power. This is demonstrated when, each day that fallen soldiers are remembered, the motives that led the now heroes to die are never remembered. One abstracts and decontexualizes in order to consolidate the symbol and confer upon it an absolutely natural character. It may be that just wars exist (like an action of defense or of liberation), but even so it remains impossible to think that *all* wars are just or holy. Then, why is this perturbing element abstracted from the collective conscience? Any questioning is (must be) interpreted as an affront to the "fallen heroes." In this way, the benefit is quadruple: 1) society washes its sins and its bad conscience; 2) the victims of the absurd receive a moral gratification and meaning for their own disgrace; 3) any radical questioning of the sense of past wars is prevented; and 4) a loan is secured against stock for wars yet to come—for a few but in the name of all.

(2005)

An Imperial Democracy

Judging by the documents that remain to us, Thucydides (460-396 B.C.) was the first philosopher in history to discover power as a human phenomenon and not as a virtue conferred by the heavens or demons. He was also aware of the principal value of money in defeating the enemy in any war. We can add another: Thucydides never believed in the principle that those with no trust in arguments are so fond of repeating in revisionist criticism: "I know what I am talking about because I lived it." We once noted that this idea was easily destroyed with two contradictory observations by those who experienced the same event. Thucydides demonstrated it thusly: "Investigation has been laborious because the witnesses have not given the same versions of the same deeds, but according to their sympathies for some and for others or they followed the memory of each one." (Ed. Gredos, Madrid 1990, p. 164)

According to Thucydides, in order for Sparta, the other great city state, to go to war against the dominant Athens, the Corinthians directed themselves to their assembly with a portrait of the great enemy democracy: "they [the Athenians] are innovators, resolute in the conception and execution of their projects; you tend to leave things as they are, to say nothing and to not even carry out that which is necessary" (236). Then: "exactly as it happens in techniques, novelties always impose themselves." (238)

Hearing of this speech, the Athenian ambassadors responded with the following words: "by the very exercise of command we saw ourselves obligated from the beginning to take the empire into the present situation, first out of fear, then out of honor, and finally out of interest; and once we were already hated by the majority [...] it did not seem safe to run the risk of letting go." (244) The law that the weaker be oppressed by the stronger has always prevailed; we believe, besides, that we are worthy of this empire, and that we appeared so to you until now, calculating your interests, you set about invoking reasons of justice, reasons that no one has ever set forth who might obtain something by force in order to stop increasing their possessions. [...] in any case, we believe that if others occupied our place, they would make perfectly clear how moderate we are"; (246) "if you were to defeat us and take control of the empire, you would quickly lose the sympathy which you have attracted thanks to the fear that we inspire." (249)

Its pride provoked, the conservative and xenophobic Sparta decides to confront Athenian expansionism. The Athenians, convinced by Pericles, refuse to negotiate and face by themselves a war that leads them to catastrophe. "We should not lament for the houses and for the land—advises Pericles, repeating a well-known topic of the period—but for the people: these goods do not obtain men, but rather it is men who obtain goods." (370)

Nonetheless, the war spreads death over Greece. In a funeral speech, Pericles (Book II) gives us testimony of the ideals and representations of the ancient Greeks, which today we would call "humanist precepts." Referring to the Spartan custom of expelling any foreigner from their land, Pericles finds a moral contrast: "our city is open to the whole world, and in no case do we turn to expulsions of foreigners" (451) In another speech he completes this ideological portrait, repeating ideas already formulated by other philosophers of Athens and which today's conservatives have forgotten: "a city that progresses collectively turns out to be more useful to individual interests than another that has prosperity in each one of its citizens, but is being ruined as a state. Because a man whose private affairs go well, if his fatherland is destroyed, he goes equally to ruin with it, while he who is unfortunate in a fortunate city is saved much more easily." (484)

But humanist egalitarian that Pericles was, he did not escape from oppressive patriotism. As if Greek foresight about society and "human nature" had become myopia by extending the gaze beyond the limits of his own homeland. Radical democracy at home becomes imperialism abroad: "Realize that she [Athens] enjoys the greatest renown among all men for not succumbing to disgrace and for having expended in war more lives and effort than any other; know that she also possesses the greatest power achieved until our days, whose memory, even though we now may come to cede a little (since everything has been born in order to diminish), will endure forever in future generations; it will be remembered that it is we Greeks who have exercised our dominion over the greatest number of Greeks, who have sustained the greatest wars against both coalitions and separate cities, and who have inhabited the richest city in every kind of resources and the largest. [...] To be hated and prove a nuisance for the moment is what has always happened to those who have attempted to dominate others; but whomever exposes himself to envy for the noblest motives takes the correct decision." (491)

In his critical introduction to this same Gredos edition, Julio Calogne Ruiz recalls that Sparta's objective was "to put an end to the progressive increase of the Athenians' markedly imperialist power. Given that all of Athens' power came from the tributes of its subjects, the pretext that Sparta gave to go to war was the liberation of all Greek cities." (20) Then he speculates: "many ordinary Athenians must have realized that their well-being basically depended on the continuity of domination over the allies without thinking about whether this was just or unjust." (26)

"The question of power in the Fifth Century is"—continues Calogne Ruiz—"the question of the imperialism of Athens. For three quarters of a century Athens is an empire and nothing in Athenian life can be removed from that reality." (80)

Nonetheless, this reality, which at times is explicitly named by Thucydides, is never expressed as a central theme in the major works of ancient thought and literature.

In *The World, the Text, and the Critic* Edward Said, referring to the literature of recent centuries, reflects on the false political neutrality of culture and the so-called "absolute freedom" of literary creation: "What such ideas mask, mystify, is precisely the network binding writers to the State and to a world-wide 'metropolitan' imperialism that, at the moment they were writing, furnished them in the novelistic techniques of narration. [...] What we must ask is why so few 'great' novelists deal directly with the major social and economic outside facts of their existence—colonialism and imperialism—and why, too, critics of the novel have continued to honor this remarkable silence."

(2004)

US Politics and Economics: The Patriotism of the Rich

Almost nowhere in the world do the rich emigrate. They rarely form part of the armies that they send off to wars, and that they then shower with honors and applause, and they curse the state that sucks their blood. When the economy is doing well, they demand tax cuts to maintain prosperity, and when things do badly they demand that the accursed state bail them out—with tax money, of course.

Since the financial crisis of 2008, the US middle class has been worried about the deficit and unemployment, both inherited from the Republican government of George W. Bush. Within this party, the splinter known as the Tea Party has risen with such force as to dominate the discourse, but which could spell the ruin of the Republican Party's chances to win an election, which in principle would seem in their favor. Their banner is the Reagan-Thatcher ideology and opposition to any tax increases. They assure us that it is wrong to penalize the successful, the rich, with taxes, since it is the rich who create jobs when the riches trickle down from above. In a debate in 2008, Obama noted that those who propose this theory (or rather, this ideology) learned when the crisis struck, that when one waits for the riches to trickle down from the top, the pain starts rising up from the bottom.

Contemporary data—to go no further—contradicts the "trickle down" theory which was taken to extremes by the last Republican government, since (1) the avarice of those on top has no limits, it is infinite, and (2) unemployment has not decreased in the last few years, on the contrary it has risen.

Even though the 700.000 jobs that were lost every month during the last year of George Bush administration has not continued after him, the creation of new jobs is extremely weak (between 15.000 and 250.000 monthly; a healthy rhythm to bring down the 9.2 per cent of unemployment would require 300.000 new jobs every month).

On the other hand, during the last year productivity has increased at much greater rates, and above all, the profit levels of the big companies. Each week one can read in the specialized press the results of a financial, industrial or service giant that has increased profits by 30, 50 or 60 per cent, as something perfectly normal, even routine. Any of these percentages come to several billion dollars. This even includes the once fallen automotive industries of Detroit. Without going into detail about how the middle class, with the State as mediator, financed the rescue of these giants, without an election and under the threat that if this were not done, worse things would happen.

Since the 1980s, wealth continues to accumulate at the top while unemployment, since 2009, continues at historic levels. Studies have demonstrated that the gap between rich and poor (Bureau of Economic Analysis), a characteristic of Latin American economies, has grown significantly under the trickle-down ideology.

Long before the crisis of 2008, when there was still a surplus inherited from the Clinton administration, the Republicans managed to lower taxes for the richest sectors of the economy, among others the oil companies. This period of grace is to end this year and was extended by Obama under pressure from the Republicans, shortly after the Democrats lost control of the House of Representatives. At that time Obama was strongly criticized from within his own party for granting concessions to the Republicans without gaining anything in return.

Nevertheless, in recent weeks the positions have polarized. In one of the last meetings with Republicans, Obama, who never loses his cool, stood up to them with the threat: "don't try me."

Faced with negotiations to increase the debt limit (a normal practice in the United States and in many other countries; the Bush administration had done this seven times) the Republicans continue to attempt to suspend and eliminate various social programs even as they reject any rise in taxes to the richest citizens (in many cases, billionaires).

On their part, the Democrats and President Obama oppose the reduction of social services and demand an increase in taxes for the very wealthy. I have heard a few millionaires asking why they shouldn't pay more taxes when it is they who have more to contribute when the country needs it. When the country from the middle on down is in need, we might point out. But apparently these millionaires are not the ones who lobby the legislatures of the rich countries.

In any event, in spite of all this Republican *mise-en-scène*, I have no doubt that before the second of August Congress will vote to raise the debt limit. Why? Because this is good for the gods of Wall Street. Not because there are unemployed workers or soldiers without legs hoping for help from the State that sent them to the front in exchange for some speeches and a few medals.

(2009)

The millionaire's union

It's a thousand times easier and more effective to believe that the working-class people of the world owe all their social justice and material progress to a handful of multimillionaires than to believe that global warming and the disappearance of insect species have been caused by human beings.

It's a thousand times easier and more effective to organize a strike for more capital than a strike on behalf of workers.

It's a thousand times easier to organize a union of millionaires for pressuring working-class people and governments at every whim than to form a union of teachers, of workers, of supermarket employees or of rural laborers. When a worker doesn't like his work or his salary, he is free to leave without his job and his salary and go somewhere else. When an investor doesn't like the work other people do or the salary they receive, he is free to leave with his money and go somewhere else.

In countries where things are upside-down, it's because the strike for more capital has already taken place on a massive scale and the country has been bankrupted or hounded by those who run the economic system that rules over the rest of us.

In countries where things are upside-down, floods are to blame for the rain and workers are to blame for the sufferings and crises of the wider society.

In this world, no government that promotes the general welfare and the social solidarity of programs for education, health or equitable development can have any chance at continuity and economic growth if it doesn't clarify beforehand its recognition of the sanctity of transnational interests and their scribes.

In this world, no government that promotes the general welfare can have any chance at continuity and economic growth if it doesn't first bow the knee before those investors who responsibly play with billions (of dollars and people) just as they responsibly drink whiskey and responsibly grab the ass of a hotel employee.

No government which recognizes that all social and economic progress in the present world hasn't been produced by a handful of successful millionaires but rather by centuries of social struggles and thousands of contributions from men and women of thought and from modest geniuses of science and technology, almost always wage-earning, has any possibility of continuity.

In this world, all governments, whether of the right or the left, whether on top or on the bottom, must protect, just like rabid dogs, the absolute freedom of capital to land in their countries and to fly to its safe havens whenever it wishes to do so, which is always when societies get the idea of making some kind of demand about their role in the investment process. And that's when societies go bankrupt and working-class people understand that they live better by living off handouts.

Which is to say that big capital shouldn't just be worshipped in practice and in fairy tales but, through private law, should also be guaranteed the right to commit extortion on a universal scale.

It goes without saying that this system -- organized and governed by a handful of multimillionaires, by founding fathers and protectors of progress in each country (developed or underdeveloped, successful or ruined), by self-sacrificing parental figures and misunderstood defenders of humanity, of an irresponsible humanity -- isn't democratic in the slightest.

And for that very reason, Liberty and Democracy are their banners, the very same flags they have fluttering like pendulums before the glazed eyes of the working class, who afterwards will gather as a lynch mob against those who don't agree with this state of collective hypnosis.

(2009)

OSAMA AND THE DANGERS OF TUNNEL VISION

Without meaning to do so, in 1690 the famous Mexican poet Sor Juana Inés de la Cruz demonstrated, with her life and death, that a person can be terribly censored by means of the very publication of her own texts. Something similar could be said for the censorship of the media. It isn't necessary to silence someone in order to censor her. Nobody prohibits a fan from yelling in a stadium filled with people, but neither is anyone, or hardly anyone, going to listen to her. If she had something important to say or yell out, it would be the same or practically the same situation as for someone who has been gagged in a silent room.

Something similar happens with regard to the importance of every global event. In this century, it is almost impossible to have a twentieth-century-style dictatorship, whether we are talking about an absolute dictatorship led by some general in some banana republic or a in a great country like the United States or the Soviet Union where there were different ideas about freedom of expression; in one, the State owned the truth and the news; in the other, the millionaires and the operators of the great media chains were the owners of almost all freedom of expression.

With the arrival and practical installation of the Digital Age, those models of censorship also became obsolete, but censorship itself did not. Individuals demanded and, in many cases, obtained a certain level of participation in the discussion of the important topics of the day. Except that now they seem like that soccer fan who yells out in the middle of a roaring stadium. Her voice and her virtual words are lost in oceans of other voices and other words. From time to time, almost always because of some kind of relevant frivolity such as the ability to lick your own elbow or owing to the unique distinction of writing the worst song in the world or coming up with the best conspiracy theory (impossible to either prove or disprove), some people get a sudden and fleeting taste of the fifteen minutes of fame that Andy Warhol talked about. I have always suspected that conspiracy theories are created and promoted by those who are supposedly implicated by them. As one of my characters in the novel *Memorias de un desaparecido* (*Memoirs of a Missing Person*, 1996) says, "There is no better strategy against a true rumor than to invent yet another false one that claims to confirm it."

But of course, this theory about a "conspiracy factory" nonetheless still belongs to the same genre of conspiracy theories. The mechanism and the deception are based upon a premise: for every one thousand conspiracy theories, one is, or must be, true.

Once theory X has entered the public discourse, it cannot be suppressed. The best thing to do is to make it disappear in a sea of superficially similar absurdities.

For now, let's put aside the matter of whether or not there is a group, government or agency responsible for manipulating perspectives worldwide (which is the same thing as manipulating reality itself). We'll assume that our common reality is a collective creation that we all participate in, like a macro-culture, like a civilization or like a supernatural system that tends to receive different names, some of them quite shopworn.

Instead, we can concentrate on the facts. For example, one fact is that, just like at any other period in history, "we are the good guys and they are the bad guys," which justifies our brutal course of action or explains why we are victims of the system in question.

But if we return to the specific matter of censorship (one of the main instruments of any dominant power), we will see that in our time a possible form of it, highly and devastatingly effective, has remained: the promotion of "what's important."

One quick and recent example is the death or assassination of Osama bin Laden. I must admit that, like other writers, I did not decline to respond to radio interviews broadcast from several countries and even in various languages. In every case, this was more as a gesture of goodwill than as an expression of personal conviction. However, this time I refrained from writing on the topic.

In my modest opinion, it appears that once more the mechanism of contemporary censorship has been employed—the excess of discussion, and the passion with which differing sides dispute the truth regarding a topic, have robbed us of the ability to concentrate on other topics. Above all, these factors keep us from appreciating how much more important certain topics are than others. It's as if someone or something decided what is important and what is not, like someone or something deciding what style or what color of clothing must be worn during a particular season.

For example, there was no means of communication by which journalists, readers and interested persons of all types, skin colors and nationalities might, over a period of weeks, passionately debate the legitimacy of bin Laden's execution. Of course, everything can and should be taken into account. But even though this kind of debate is legitimate, it becomes tragic on a global scale when we observe that the focus of attention *has determined and defined what is important.* However, does it matter whether or not a harmful character (fictitious or real) such as bin Laden was properly or improperly executed, when the undeniable facts are not even mentioned: the murder of children and other innocent persons as customary collateral damages?

In the case of bin Laden's execution, at least this time the United States proceeded in truly surgical fashion, as has been falsely proclaimed on other occasions. The lives of the children who dwelt in the house were obviously safeguarded beyond the moment of what was for them a traumatic experience. Beyond the fact that this option was necessarily strategic rather than humanitarian, let us not forget that only a few years or months ago, the standard decision was to bomb the objective without concern for "collateral damage," that is, without attaching any importance to the presence of innocent persons, quite often children. This tragedy has been so common throughout contemporary history that the affected authorities have done little more than demand better explanations for ever more horrible atrocities before tossing them into the dustbin of our collective forgetfulness.

To avoid taking this topic too far, it would be enough to mention the recent NATO bombing of Libyan dictator (or whatever you want to call him) Muammar Qaddafi. As a consequence of this bombing, the "objective" did not die. The so-called surgical operation killed—assassinated—several people, among them Qaddafi's son and three of his grandchildren. But whether or not you can believe it, these children had names and ages: Saif, 2 years; Carthage, 3 years; Mastura, 4 months. Even worse, they are not the exception—they are the rule.

Who remembers their names? Who cares?

There are no relativisms in this: a child is an innocent being regardless of circumstances, identity, religion, ideology or any action committed by her parents. A child is always—always—innocent, and is such without any qualifiers, no matter how much they may cause us, their parents, to lose patience with them time and time again.

If the police forces of any of our civilized countries were to toss a bomb into the house of the worst murderer or worst rapist of all, and by doing so kill three children, there would surely be a popular outcry in that country. If the government had given the order for such a procedure, it would surely fall in less than twenty-four hours and the persons responsible would be brought before meticulous courts of law.

But since the same thing was done to children belonging to supposedly barbarous, savage and backwards peoples, then the action is simply converted into "collateral damage," and those who carried it out are valued as responsible and valiant leaders who defend civilization, freedom, and most definitely the lives of the innocent.

And in order to keep this discussion from taking priority over all other discussions, somebody or something decides that what is really important is to have a discussion about the manner in which an individual was executed, or the legitimacy of his execution—an individual whose actions, it is supposed, had sufficiently merited the way he met his end.

(2010)

Ron Paul and Right-Wing Anarchism

Scandalized by the misery that he had encountered in the poorer classes of the powerful French nation, Thomas Jefferson wrote to Madison, informing him that this was the consequence of the "unequal division of property." France's wealth, thought Jefferson, was concentrated in very few hands, which caused the masses to be unemployed and forced them to beg. He also recognized that "the equal distribution of property is impracticable," but acknowledged that marked differences led to misery. If one wanted to preserve the utopian project for liberty in America, no longer for reasons of justice only, it was urgently necessary to insure that the laws would divide the properties obtained through inheritance so that they might be equally distributed among descendants (Bailyn 2003, 57). Thus, in 1776 Jefferson abolished the laws in his state that privileged inheritors, and established that all adult persons who did not possess 50 acres of land would receive them from the state, since "the land belongs to the living, not the dead" (58).

Jefferson once expressed his belief that if he had to choose between a government without newspapers and newspapers without a government, he would choose the latter. Like the majority of his founding peers, he was famous for other libertarian ideas, for his moderate anarchism, and for an assortment of other contradictions.

Ron Paul: Carrying Jefferson's torch in a hostile environment?

Maybe nowadays Ron Paul is a type of postmodern incarnation of that president and erudite philosopher. Perhaps for that same reason he has been displaced by Sarah Palin as representing the definition of what it means to be a supposedly good conservative. In addition to being a medical doctor, a representative for Texas, and one of the historic leaders of the Libertarian movement, Paul is probably the true founder of the non-existent Tea Party.

If anything has differentiated neoconservative Republicans from liberal Democrats during the last few decades, it has been the former's strong international interventionism with messianic influences or its tendency to legislate against homosexual marriage. On the other hand, if anything has characterized the strong criticism and legislative practice of Ron Paul, it has been his proposal to eliminate the central bank of the United States, his opposition to the meddling of the state in the matter of defining what is or should be a marriage, and his opposition to all kinds of interventionism in the affairs of other nations.

A good example of this was the Republican Party debate in Miami in December of 2007. While the rest of the candidates dedicated themselves to repeating prefabricated phrases that set off rounds of applause and stoked the enthusiasm of Miami's Hispanic community, Ron Paul did not lose the opportunity to repeat his discomforting convictions.

In response to a question from María Elena Salinas about how to deal with the president of Venezuela, Ron Paul simply answered that he was in favor of having a dialogue with Chavez and with Cuba. Of course, the boos echoed throughout the venue. Without waiting for the audience to calm down, he came back with: "But let me tell you why, why we have problems in Central and South America—because we've been involved in their internal affairs for a long time, we've gotten involved in their business. We created the Chavezes of this world, we've created the Castros of this world by interfering and creating chaos in their countries and they've responded by taking out their elected leaders…"

The boos ended with the Texan's argumentative line, until they asked him again about the war in Iraq: "We didn't have a reason to get involved there, we didn't declare war […] I have a different point of view because I respect the Constitution and I listen to the founding fathers, who told us to stay out of the internal affairs of other nations."

In matters of its internal politics, the Libertarian movement shares various points with the neoconservatives, for example, the idea that inequalities are a consequence of freedom among different individuals with different skills and interests. Hence, the idea of "wealth distribution" is understood by Ron Paul's followers as an arbitrary act of social injustice. For other neocons, it is simply an outcome of the ideological indoctrination of socialists like Obama. Subsequently, they never lose the opportunity to point out all of the books by Karl Marx that Obama studied, apparently with a passionate interest, at Columbia University, and all of the "Socialist Scholars Conference" meetings that he attended (*Radical-in-Chief: Barack Obama and the Untold Story of American Socialism*, Stanley Kurtz). Nonetheless, according to the perspective of the libertarians, all of this would fall within the rights of anyone, such as smoking marijuana, as long as one doesn't try to impose it upon everyone else, which in a president would be at the very least a difficult proposition.

The sacred cow of neoconservative North Americans is liberty (since according to them liberalism is a bad word), as if it had to do with an exalted concept separate from reality. In order to attain it, it would be enough to do away with or reduce everything called state and government, with the exception of the military. Hence, the strong inclination of some people for keeping guns in the hands of individuals, so that they can be used against meddling government power, whether their own or that of others. Fanatics for total liberty either do not consider or minimize the fact that in order to be free, a certain amount of power is needed. According to Jefferson and Che Guevara, money was only a necessary evil, an outcome of corruption in society and a frequent instrument of robbery. However, in our time (the Greeks in the era of Pericles already knew this), power stems from money. It is enough, then, to have more money in order to be—in social rather than existential terms—freer than a worker who cannot make use of the same degree of liberty to educate his children or to have free time for encouraging his own personal development and intellectual creativity.

At the other extreme, in a large part of Latin America, these days the sacred cow is the "redistribution of wealth" by means of the state. The fact that production can also be poorly distributed is often not considered or is frequently minimized. In this case, the cultural parameters are crucial—there are individuals and groups who create and work for others, who in turn cry out because of the injustice of not getting the benefits that they would deserve if social justice existed. Which is like a liar who hides behind a truth in order to safeguard and perpetuate his vices. According to this position, any merit is only the outcome of an oppressive system that doesn't even allow the idle to put their idleness behind them. So, idleness and robbery are explained by the economic structure and the culture of oppression that keeps entire groups shrouded in ignorance. Which up to a certain point is not untrue. However, it is not sufficient proof of the non-existence of perpetual bums and others who are barely equipped for physical or intellectual work. In any case, there should not be redistribution of wealth if there is not first redistribution of production, which would partly be a redistribution of the desire to study, work and take on responsibility for something.

These days, states are necessary evils for protecting equa-liberty, equality and liberty. But at the same time, they are the main instrument, as those revolutionary Americans believed, for protecting the privileges of the most powerful and for feeding the moral vices of the weakest.

(2010)

Hurricane Katrina and the Hyperreality of the Image

In the 16th century, the Dominican brother Bartolomé de las Casas wrote an impassioned chronicle about the brutal conquest by the Spanish Empire of the new world. The denunciation by this Christian convert (which is to say, "of impure blood") in behalf of a universal humanism, resulted in the Juntas de Valladolid (1550) in which he faced off, before the public and the king, with Ginés de Sepúlveda. Using a biblical quotation taken from Proverbs, Juan Ginés de Sepúlveda and his partisans defended the right of the Empire to enslave indigenous peoples, not only because they did it in the name of the "true faith" but, above all, because the Bible said that the intelligent man must subjugate the idiot. We will not go into who were the intelligent men. What matters now is knowing that over the centuries, a debate resulted among the "chroniclers" (the only literary genre permitted by the Spanish Inquisition in the Americas). As always, only a minority promoted a new ethics based on ethical "principles." In this case the humanists and defenders of the "natural right" of the indigenous peoples. One had to wait until the 19th century for these "principles" to become reality by the force of "necessity." In other words, the Industrial Revolution needed wage laborers, not free labor that competed with standardized production and that, besides, had no consumption power. From that point on, as always, "necessity" quickly universalized the "principles," so that today we all consider ourselves "anti-slavery," based on ethical "principles" and not by "necessity."[1] I have explained this elsewhere, but what is important to me now is to briefly analyze the power of the written text and, beyond this, the power of dialectical (and sometimes sophistic) analysis.

Using the denunciations of father Bartolomé de las Casas, a nascent empire (the British) quickly found writers to create the "black legend" of Spain's colonial enterprise. Then, like any new empire, it presumed an advanced morality: it presented itself as the champion of the anti-slavery struggle (which—what a coincidence—only became a reality when its industries developed in the 19th century) and pretended to give moral lessons without the necessary authority, which was denied by its own history of brutal oppression, equally as brutal as that of the old Spanish empire.

---

[1] This same principle that I call "necessity" was identified in the 19th century by Bautista Alberdi, when he recognized that laicism in the Rio de la Plata was (and had to be) a consequence of the great diversity of religions, a product of immigration. It was not possible to expel or engage in "ethnic cleansing," as Spain did in the 15th century, since in Alberdi's time we were in a different arena of history, and of the concept of "necessary resources."

Shortly after the De las Casas-Supúlveda controversy and following the approval of the New Laws governing treatment of the Indians as a consequence (although the laws weren't worth the paper they were printed on), Guamán Poma Ayala denounced a similar history of rapes, torture and mass murder. But he did it, in contrast, with a collection of drawings, which at the time was a form of chronicle as valid as the written word. These drawings can be studied in detail today, but we would have to say that their impact and interest was minimal in their own time, despite the starkness of the images. In those days, just as during the Middle Ages, images had a special usefulness because the majority of the population did not know how to read. Nevertheless, and for that very reason, it is easy to explain why Guamán Poma's chronicle was of no great consequence: because the "masses," the population, didn't matter as an agent of change. Or it simply didn't matter. Rebellion might be headed by a cacique, like Tupac Amaru, but the population was not a protagonist of its own story.

Now here's where I'm going with this: this process has been reversed today. The "masses" are no longer "masses" and have begun to matter: citing Ortega y Gasset, we might say that we had a "rebellion of the masses" but now can longer speak of "masses" but of a population composed of individuals that have started to question, to make demands, and to rebel. Nonetheless, the struggle is rooted on this front: as the masses (now subjects in rebellion) matter in the generation of the story, those who still belong to the old order seek to dominate them with their own language:

the image. And often they succeed to perfection. Let's take a look.

Our Western popular culture is based (at times trapped) in visual codes and a visual sensibility. We know that the culture of the ruling (or dominant) classes continues to be based on the complexities of the written text. Even the experts on images base their studies and theories on the written word. If in Latin America public opinion and sensibility are strongly conditioned by an ideological tradition (formed from the time of the Conquest, in the 16th century, and exploited by opposing political groups in the 20th century), here, in the United States, the relationship with the past is less conflict-oriented, and hence the lack of historical memory can, in some cases, facilitate the work of the proselytizers. We will not get into that issue here. Suffice it to say that the United States is a complex and contradictory country, and therefore any judgement about "Americanness" is as arbitrary and unfair as speaking of "Latinamericanness" without recognizing the great diversity that exists within that mythological construct. We must not forget that all ideology (of the left or of the right, liberal or conservative) sustains itself via a strategic simplification of the reality it analyzes or creates.

I understand that these factors should be taken into account when we want to understand why the image is a basic "text" for capitalist societies: its "consumption" is quick, disposable, and therefore "comfortable." The problem arises when this image (the sign, the text) ceases to be comfortable and pleasant. When this happens the public reacts, becomes aware. That is to say, the understanding, the awareness, enters through the eyes: a photograph of a girl fleeing the napalm bombs in Viet Nam, for example. For the same reason it was "recommended" to not show the public images of the war in Iraq that included children torn apart by bombs (see the daily papers of the rest of the world in 2003), the coffins of American soldiers returning home, etc. By contrast, the Terri Schiavo case occupied the time and concern of the American public for many weeks, day after day, hour after hour; the president and governor Bush of Florida signed "exceptions" that were rejected by the judiciary, until the poor woman died to rest in peace from so many obscene images of which she was the unknowing and unwilling victim. Despite it all, during those same weeks hundreds of Iraqis, as well as American soldiers, continued to die and they didn't even make the news, beyond the publication of the daily statistic. Why? Because they aren't persons, they are numbers for a sensibility that is only moved by images. And this was proved by the photographs of Abu Graib and with a video that showed an American soldier shooting a wounded man. Those were the only two moments in which the American public reacted with indignation. But we should ask ourselves, does anyone really believe that these things don't happen in war? Does anyone still believe in that postmodern story about hygienic wars, where there are "special effects" but no blood, death and pain? Yes. Many people do. Lamentably, a majority. And it's not due to lack of intelligence but to lack of interest.

We can analyze the same process at work with the recent problem of New Orleans. The catastrophe was not grasped when the meteorologists warned of the scale of the tragedy, several days before. Nor was there broad awareness of the problem when reports spoke of tens of dead. Four days after, we knew that the number of dead could rise into the hundreds. Possibly thousands, if we consider those who will die for lack of dialysis, lack of insulin and other emergency medicines. But television did not show a single dead person. Anyone can search the pages of the principal daily newspapers of the United States and they will not find an "offensive" image, one of those photographs that we can view in daily papers from other parts of the world: bodies floating, children dying "like in Africa," violence, rapes, etc. Because if there is one thing in abundance it is digital cameras; but there is even more "modesty." I am no advocate of morbid gratuitousness, nor of showing blood over and over again unnecessarily: I am an advocate of showing everything. As a U.S. citizen said with reference to the war, "if we were capable of doing it we should be capable of seeing it."

A natural tragedy like this one (or like the tsunami in Asia) is a disgrace for which we cannot hold anyone responsible. (Let's set aside, for a moment, the share of responsibility that societies have in the global warming of the oceans.) Nonetheless, the tragedy of New Orleans demonstrates that a superpower like the United States can mobilize tens of thousands of soldiers, the most advanced technology in the world, the most effective machinery of assault in human history in order to remove a foreign president (or dictator), but prove incapable of reaching thousands of victims of Hurricane Katrina, in a city within its own country. In New Orleans, there were acts of vandalism and violence, rapes and general chaos while victims complained that there were no policemen or soldiers to help them, in an area that found itself under martial law. This complaint was made in front of the cameras, and so we can believe that at least the journalists were able to gain access to those places. Some loot because they are opportunists, others out of desperation, as they begin to experience a situation of struggle for survival previously not seen in the most powerful country in the world. On September 1 president G.W. Bush appealed for private aid and on September 2 he said it was not sufficient. There is no lack of resources, of course (the war in Iraq cost more than three hundred billion dollars, ten times more than all the damages produced by the hurricane in this tragedy); the Congress voted for economic aid of ten billion dollars for the victims. But the latter continued to die, trapped in stadiums, on bridges, without shelter, offering up a jarring image for a country whose poor suffer from problems of overeating, where beggars are fined a thousand dollars for asking for things they don't need (since the State supposedly provides them everything necessary to survive without desperation in case they can't do so by their own means). Undocumented Hispanics suffer a double tragedy: they will not receive compensation like their neighbors but rest assured that they will be the first to take up the task of reconstruction. Who else? What other social group in this country has the physical, moral and spiritual toughness to work under conditions of survival and hopelessness? Or do we still believe in fairy tales?

The people of the United States will become aware of the objectives and priorities of this government when they compare its efficiency or inefficiency in different places and moments. But for that to happen they must "see it" on their television sets, in the English-language news media on the Internet, to which they turn out of habit. Because it is of little or no use for them to read it in written texts, since the critical analyses of the New York Times are seemingly useless—a paper that, with a large number of brilliant analysts noting one by one the contradictions of this government, took sides publicly against the reelection of G. W. Bush. Now, when there is a "fatigue" in public opinion, the majority of the country's population understands that the intervention in Iraq was a mistake. Of course, as my grandfather used to say, you chirped too late.

U.S. public opinion will become aware of what is happening in New Orleans (and of what is happening beyond the natural phenomenon) when people can see images; a part of what the victims see and tell orally to a public that listens but is unmoved by a dialectical analysis that doesn't appeal to images or biblical metaphors. The U.S. public will realize what is happening when its sees "raw" images, as long as they don't confuse those images with the chaos of some underdeveloped country.

The brilliant Brazilian educator, Paulo Freire, exiled by the dictatorship of his country "out of ignorance," published in 1971 *The Pedagogy of the Oppressed* with a publishing house in Montevideo, Uruguay. He mentioned there the pedagogical experience of a colleague. The teacher had shown to a student an alley of New York City filled with garbage and asked him what he saw. The boy said that he saw a street in Africa or Latin America. "And why not a street in New York City?" observed the teacher. A short time earlier, in the 1950s, Roland Barthes had done an interesting analysis of a photograph in which a black soldier saluted "patriotically" the flag of the empire that oppressed Africa (the French empire), and concluded, among other things, that the image was conditioned by the (written) text that accompanies it and that it is the latter that confers on the image (ideological) meaning. We might think that the semantic (or semiotic) problem is a bit more complex than this, and arises from other unwritten "texts," other images, other (hegemonic) discourses, etc. But the "raw" image also has a revelatory, or at least critical, function. What do I mean by "raw"? "Raw" images are precisely those images censored (or repressed, to use a psychoanalytic term) by the dominant discourse. For this reason those of us who use dialectics and analysis related historically to thought and language must recognize, at the same time, the power of those others who control visual language. To dominate or to liberate, to hide or to reveal.

Once, in an African village, a Macua man told me how a sorceress had transformed a sack of sand into a sack of sugar, and how another sorcerer had come flying down from the sky. I asked him if he remembered any strange, recent dream. The Macua man told me he had dreamed that he saw his village from an airplane. "Have you ever flown in a plane?" I asked. Obviously not. He hadn't even been close to one of those machines. "But you say that you saw it," I observed. "Yes, but it was a dream," he told me. Spirits in the bodies of lions, flying men, sand turned into sugar aren't dreams. Stories like these can be read in the chronicles of the Spaniards who conquered Latin America in the 16th century. We can also see them today in many regions of Central America. My response to my Macua friend was the same as I would give to the more "evolved" U.S. public: we must always be aware that not everything we see is true, nor can everything true be seen.

(2005)

If Latin America Had Been a British Enterprise

In 2005, in the process of conducting a recent study at the University of Georgia, a female student interviewed a young Colombian woman and tape-recorded the interview. The young woman commented on her experience in England and how the British were interested in knowing the reality of Colombia. After she detailed the problems that her country had, one Englishman observed the paradox that England, despite being smaller and possessing fewer natural resources, was much wealthier than Colombia. His conclusion was cutting: "If England had managed Colombia like a business, Colombians today would be much richer."

The Colombian youth admitted her irritation, because the comment was intended to point out just how incapable we are in Latin America. The lucid maturity of the young Colombian woman was evident in the course of the interview, but in that moment, she could not find the words to respond to the son of the old empire. The heat of the moment, the audacity of those British kept her from remembering that in many respects Latin America had indeed been managed like a British enterprise and that, therefore, the idea was not only far from original but, also, was part of the reason that Latin America was so poor—with the caveat that poverty is a scarcity of capital and not of historical consciousness.

Agreed: three hundred years of monopolistic, retrograde and frequently cruel colonization has weighed heavily upon the Latin American continent, and consolidated in the spirit of our nations an oppositional psychology with respect to social and political legitimation (Alberto Montaner called that cultural trait "the suspicious original legitimacy of power"). Following the semi-independences of the 19th century, the "progress" of the British railroad system was not only a kind of gilded cage—in the words of Eduardo Galeano -, a straight-jacket for native Latin American development, but we can see something similar in Africa: in Mozambique, for example, a country that extends North-to-South, the roads cut across it from East-to-West. The British Empire was thus able to extract the wealth of its central colonies by passing through the Portuguese colony. In Latin America we can still see the networks of asphalt and steel flowing together toward the ports—old bastions of the Spanish colonies that native rebels contemplated with infinite rancor from the heights of the savage sierras, and which the large land owners saw as the maximum progress possible for countries that were backward by "nature."

Obviously, these observations do not exempt us, the Latin Americans, from assuming our own responsibilities. We are conditioned by an economic infrastructure, but not determined by it, just as an adult is not tied irremediably to the traumas of childhood. Certainly, we must confront these days other kinds of strait-jackets, conditioning imposed on us from outside and from within, by the inevitable thirst for dominance of world powers who refuse strategic change, on the one hand, and frequently by our own culture of immobility, on the other. For the former it is necessary to lose our innocence; for the latter we need the courage to criticize ourselves, to change ourselves and to change the world.

(2005)

On How to Topple an Empire

The same day that Christopher Columbus left the port of Palos, the third of August of 1492, was the deadline for the Jews of Spain to leave their country. In the admiral's mind there were at least two powerful goals, two irrefutable truths: the material riches of Asia and the perfect religion of Europe. With the former he intended to finance the reconquest of Jerusalem; with the latter he would legitimate the looting. The word "oro," Spanish for "gold," spilled from his pen in the same way the divine and bloody metal spilled from the ships of the conquistadors who followed him. That same year, the second of January of 1492, Granada had fallen, the last Arab bastion on the Iberian Peninsula. 1492 was also the year of the publication of the first Castilian grammar (the first European grammar in a "vulgar" language). According to its author, Antonio de Nebrija, language was the "companion to empire." Immediately, the new power continued the Reconquest with the Conquest, on the other side of the Atlantic, using the same methods and the same convictions, confirming the globalizing vocation of all empires.

At the center of power there had to be a language, a religion and a race. Future Spanish nationalism would be built on the foundation of a cleansing of memory. It is true that eight centuries before Jews and Aryan Visigoths had called for and later helped Muslims replace Roderick and the rest of the Visigoth kings who had fought for the same purification. But this was not the principal reason for despising the Jews, because it was not memory that was important but forgetting. The Catholic monarchs and successive divine royalty finished off (or wanted to) the other Spain, multicultural and mestizo Spain, the Spain where several languages were spoken and several religions were practiced and several races mixed. The Spain that had been the center of culture, the arts and the sciences, in a Europe submerged in backwardness, in the violent superstitions and provincialism of the Middle Ages. More and more, the Iberian Peninsula began closing its borders to difference. Moors and Jews had to abandon their country and emigrate to Barbaria (Africa) or to the rest of Europe, where they integrated to peripheral nations that emerged with new economic, social and intellectual restlessness.[2] Within the borders were left some illegitimate children, African slaves who go almost unmentioned in the better known version of history but

---

[2] It is commonly said that the Renaissance began with the fall of Constantinople and the emigration of Greek intellectuals to Italy, but little or nothing is said of the emigration of knowledge and capital that were forced to abandon Spain.

who were necessary for undignified domestic tasks. The new and successful Spain enclosed itself in a conservative movement (if one will permit me the oxymoron). The state and religion were strategically united for better control of Spain's people during a schizophrenic process of purification. Some dissidents like Bartolomé de las Casas had to face, in public court, those who, like Ginés de Supúlveda, argued that the empire had the right to invade and dominate the new continent because it was written in the Bible (Proverbs 11:29) that "the foolish shall be servant to the wise of heart." The others, the subjugated, are such because of their "inferior intellect and inhumane and barbarous customs." The speech of the famous and influential theologian, sensible like all official discourse, proclaimed: "[the natives] are barbarous and inhumane peoples, are foreign to civil life and peaceful customs, and it will be just and in keeping with natural law that such peoples submit to the empire of more cultured and humane nations and princes, so that due to their virtues and the prudence of their laws such peoples might throw off their barbarism and reduce themselves to a more humane life and worship of virtue." And in another moment: "one must subjugate by force of arms, if by other means is not possible, those who by their natural condition must obey others but refuse to submit." At the time one did not take recourse to words like "democracy" and "freedom" because until the 19th century these remained in Spain attributes of humanist chaos, anarchy and the devil. But each imperial power in each moment of history plays the same game with different cards. Some, as one can see, not so different.

Despite an initially favorable reaction from King Carlos V and the New Laws that prohibited enslavement of native Americans (Africans were not considered subject to rights), the empire, through its propertied class, continued enslaving and exterminating those peoples considered "foreign to civil life and peaceful customs" in the name of salvation and humanization. In order to put an end to the horrible Aztec rituals that periodically sacrificed an innocent victim to their pagan gods, the empire tortured, raped and murdered en masse, in the name of the law and of the one, true God. According to Bartolomé de las Casas, one of the methods of persuasion was to stretch the savages over a grill and roast them alive. But it was not only torture—physical and moral—and forced labor that depopulated lands that at one time had been inhabited by thousands of people; weapons of mass destruction were also employed, biological weapons to be more specific. Smallpox and the flu decimated entire populations unintentionally at times, and according to precise calculation on other occasions. As the English had discovered to the north, sometimes the delivery of contaminated gifts, like the clothing of infected people, or the dumping of pestilent cadavers, had more devastating effects than heavy artillery.

Now, who defeated one of the greatest empires in history, the Spanish Empire? Spain. As a conservative mentality, cutting across all social classes, clung to a belief in its divine destiny, as the "armed hand of God" (according to Menéndez Pelayo), the empire sank into its own past. The society of empire fractured and the gap separating the rich from the poor grew at the same time that the empire guaranteed the mineral resources (precious metals in this case) allowing it to function. The poor increased in number and the rich increased the wealth they accumulated in the name of God and country. The empire had to finance the wars that it maintained beyond its borders and the fiscal deficit grew until it became a monster out of control. Tax cuts mainly benefited the upper classes, to such an extent that they often were not even required to pay them or were exempted from going to prison for debt or embezzlement. The state went bankrupt several times. Nor was the endless flow of mineral resources coming from its colonies, beneficiaries of the enlightenment of the Gospel, sufficient: the government spent more than what it received from these invaded lands, requiring it to turn to the Italian banks.

This is how, when many countries of America (what is now called Latin America) became independent, there was no longer anything left of the empire but its terrible reputation. Fray Servando Teresa de Mier wrote in 1820 that if Mexico had not yet become independent it was because of the ignorance of the people, who did not yet understand that the Spanish Empire was no longer an empire, but the poorest corner of Europe. A new empire was consolidating power, the British Empire. Like previous empires, and like those that would follow, the extension of its language and the dominance of its culture would be common factors. Another would be publicity: England did not delay in using the chronicles of Bartolomé de las Casas to defame the old empire in the name of a superior morality. A morality that nonetheless did not preclude the same kind of rape and criminality. But clearly, what matters most are the good intentions: well-being, peace, freedom, progress—and God, whose omnipresence is demonstrated by His presence in all official discourse.

Racism, discrimination, the closing of borders, messianic religious belief, wars for peace, huge fiscal deficits to finance these wars, and radical conservatism lost the empire. But all of these sins are summed up in one: arrogance, because this is the one that keeps a world power from seeing all the other ones. Or it allows them to be seen, but in distorted fashion, as if they were grand virtues.

(2004)

Propaganda and the Myth of Reconquest

A well-known syndicated talk radio personality repeatedly asserted an opinion that has been common in the last decades: illegal immigrants should be denounced as dishonest and criminal, not only because they have entered the U.S. illegally but, mainly, because their objective is the Reconquest.

Let's analyze the syllogism posited here. Even assuming that illegal workers are Reconquistadors—that's what they were called—which is to say that they lay claim to vast territories lost by Mexico to Anglo Saxon settlers in the 19th century, one would have to conclude, according to the argument of the angry sophists, that the U.S. is founded on illegitimacy and the actions of alleged criminals. (Texas was conquered in 1836 and thereby re-established slavery in a Mexican territory where it was illegal; other Western states met the same fate, following a war with Mexico and a payment to the vanquished in the manner of a purchase, because by then money was already a powerful legitimating agent.)

Now, if a reconquest is a crime, then what is a conquest? In any case it would be understandable to assert that this immigration phenomenon is not politically convenient (although economically it appears to be so). But, dishonest? Criminal? Would they dare to qualify as criminal the Spanish Reconquest of the Iberian Peninsula? No, of course not, and not because it wasn't carried out in a bloody and racist fashion, but because in that case it was a matter of Christians against Muslims—and Jews.

Any conquest, like any reconquest, is a simple political deed that aims to hide behind morality. The legitimacy of the deed always originates from force; propaganda then takes on the task of confusing force with morality, or with exposing the contradictions to analysis. In general, the propaganda is abused by the victors, and analysis is a meager resource of the vanquished. Much like today, in the Middle Ages propaganda, both religious and political, was indispensable. The nobility, the upper classes, were the ones who produced the greatest quantity of nationalist propaganda, aimed at morally orienting the people. Nevertheless, both in the early years of the Muslim conquest in Spain, and later in the Spanish conquest in the Americas, the upper classes were the first to come to an agreement with the invaders in order to maintain their class and gender privileges.

Propaganda is the hook in the jaw of history. The idea of a reconquest is a fiction for millions of expatriated workers, the forever disinherited who simply look to survive and feed their economically marginal families by recourse to a hundred-years-old, unjust, anachronistic social tradition. But it is a strategic fiction for the propagandists who are able to use it to hide the dramatic political rationale—i.e., the rationale of power—that exists behind the moralizing discourse.

Every time I hear someone preaching, I lose faith. That faith to which the haranguers of the U.S. extreme right and the *caudillos* of Latin American liberation lay claim. The more I hear, the less I believe. But this surely is the fault of my personal inability to enjoy what other people enjoy, like the safety of trenches dug with propaganda and self-indulgence.

(2006)

Racism does not need racists

In my classes, I always try to make clear the difference between opinions and facts. It is a fundamental rule, a very simple intellectual exercise that we owe ourselves to undertake in the post-Enlightenment era. I started becoming obsessed with such obvious matters when I found out, in 2005, that some students were arguing that something "is true because I believe it" – and they weren't joking. Since then, I've suspected that such intellectual conditioning, such a conflation of physics with metaphysics (cleared up by Averroes almost a thousand years ago) – which year by year becomes increasingly dominant (faith as the supreme criterion, regardless of all evidence to the contrary) – has its origins in the majestic churches of the southern United States.

But critical thinking involves so much more than just distinguishing facts from opinions. Trying to define what a fact is would suffice. The very idea of objectivity itself paradoxically originates from a single perspective, from one lens. And anyone knows that with the lens of one photographic or video camera, only one part of reality is captured, which quite often is subjective or used to distort reality in the supposed interest of objectivity.

For some reason, students tend to be more interested in opinions than facts. Maybe because of the superstitious idea that an informed opinion is derived from the synthesis of thousands of facts. This is a dangerous idea, but we can't run away from our responsibility to give our opinion when it's required. All that we can and should do is take note that an informed opinion continues to be an opinion which must be tested or challenged.

On a certain day, students discussed the caravan of 5,000 Central Americans (at least one thousands of whom were children) fleeing violence and heading for the Mexican border with the US. President Donald Trump had ordered the border closed and called those looking for refuge "invaders". On 29 October 2018, he tweeted: "This is an invasion of our Country and our Military is waiting for you!". The military deployment to the border alone cost the US about $200 million.

Since one of my students insisted on knowing my opinion, I started off with the most controversial side of the issue. I observed that this country, the US, was founded upon the fear of invasion, and only a select few have always known how to exploit this weakness, with tragic consequences. Maybe this paranoia came about with the English invasion of 1812, but if history tells us anything, it's that the US has practically never suffered an invasion of its territory – if we exclude the 9/11 attacks in 2001; the one on Pearl Harbor, which at the time was a military base in foreign territory; and, prior to that, at the very beginning of the twentieth century, the brief incursion of a Mexican named

Pancho Villa mounted upon a horse. But the US has indeed specialized in invading other countries from the time of its founding – it took over the Indian territories, then half of Mexico, from Texas, to reinstall slavery, to California; it intervened directly in Latin American affairs, to repress popular protests and support bloody dictatorships – all in the name of defense and security. And always with tragic consequences.

Therefore, the idea that a few thousand poor people on foot are going to invade the most powerful country in the world is simply a joke in poor taste. And it's likewise in bad taste for some Mexicans on the other side to adopt this same xenophobic talk that's been directed at them – inflicting on others the same abuse they've suffered.

In the course of the conversation, I mentioned in passing that in addition to the foundational paranoia, there was a racial component to the argument.

"You don't need to be a racist to defend the borders," said one student.

True, I noted. You don't need to be a racist to defend borders or laws. At first glance, the statement is irrefutable. However, if we take history and the wider current context into consideration, an openly racist pattern jumps out at us right away.

At the end of the nineteenth century, the French novelist Anatole France wrote: "The law, in its majestic equality, forbids rich and poor alike to sleep under bridges, to beg in the streets, and to steal their bread." You don't need to be an elitist to support an economically stratified culture. You don't need to be sexist to spread the most rampant type of sexism. Thoughtlessly engaging in certain cultural practices and voicing your support for some law or another is quite often all it takes.

I drew a geometric figure on the board and asked students what they saw there. Everyone said they saw a cube or a box. The most creative variations didn't depart from the idea of tri-dimensionality, when in reality what I drew was nothing more than three rhombuses forming a hexagon. Some tribes in Australia don't see that same image in 3D but rather in 2D. We see what we think and that's what we call objectivity.

When President Abraham Lincoln emerged victorious from the American Civil War (1861-1865), he put an end to a hundred-year dictatorship that, up to this day, everyone calls "democracy." By the eighteenth century, black slaves had come to make up more than fifty per cent of the population in states like South Carolina – but they weren't even citizens of the US, nor did they enjoy even minimal human rights.

Many years before Lincoln, both racists and anti-racists proposed a solution to the "negro problem" by sending them "back" to Haiti or Africa, where many of them ended up founding the nation of Liberia (one of my students, Adja, is from a family which comes from that African country). The English did the same thing to "rid" England of its blacks. But under Lincoln blacks became citizens, and one way to reduce them down to a minority was not only by making it difficult for them to vote (such as by imposing a poll tax) but also by opening the nation's borders to immigration.

The Statue of Liberty, a gift from the French people to the American people to commemorate the centenary of the 1776 Declaration of Independence, still cries with silent lips: "Give me your tired, your poor, your huddled masses yearning to breathe free..." In this way, the US opened its arms to waves of impoverished immigrants. Of course, the overwhelming majority were poor whites. Many were opposed to the Italians and the Irish because they were red-headed Catholics. But in any case, they were seen as being better than blacks. Blacks weren't able to immigrate from Africa, not just because they were much farther away than Europeans were, but also because they were much poorer, and there were hardly any shipping routes to connect them to New York. The Chinese had more opportunities to reach the west coast, and perhaps for that reason a law was passed in 1882 that prohibited them from coming in just for being Chinese.

I understand that this was a subtle and powerful way to reshape demographics, which is to say the political, social and racial make-up of the US. The current nervousness about a change to that make-up is nothing more than the continuation of that same old logic. Were that not the case, what could be wrong with being part of a minority group or being different from others?

Clearly, if you're a good person and you're in favour of properly enforcing laws, it doesn't make you a racist. You don't need to be racist when the law and the culture already are. In the

US, nobody protests Canadian or European immigrants. The same is true in Europe and even in the Southern Cone of South America (the southernmost region of Latin America, populated mainly by descendants of Europeans). But everyone is worried about the blacks and the hybrid, mixed-race people from the south. Because they're not white and "good", but poor and "bad". Currently, almost half a million European immigrants are living illegally in the United States. Nobody talks about them, just like nobody talks about how one million United States citizens are living in Mexico, many illegally.

With communism discarded as an excuse (none of those chronically failing states where migrants come from are communist), let's once again consider the racial and cultural excuses common to the century prior to the Cold War. Every dark-skinned worker is seen as a criminal, not an opportunity for mutual development. The immigration laws are themselves filled with panic at the sight of poor workers.

It's true that you don't need to be racist to support laws and more secure borders. You also don't need to be racist to spread and shore up an old racist and class-based paradigm, while we fill our mouths with platitudes about compassion and the fight for freedom and human dignity.

(2018)

The Culture of Hate

On the silent revolution and reaction of our time. The reasons for ultramodern chaos. On the colonization of language and how traditional authority reacts to historical progress using the anachronistic tools of repetition.

The old pedagogical model was synthesized in the phrase "the letters enter with blood." This was the ideological support that allowed the teacher to strike with a ruler the buttocks or hands of the bad students. When the bad student was able to memorize and repeat what the teacher wanted, the punishment would end and the reward would begin. Then the bad student, having now been turned into "a good man," could take over teaching by repeating the same methods. It is not by accident that the celebrated Argentine statist and pedagogue, F. Sarmiento, would declare "a child is nothing more than an animal that must be tamed and educated." In fact, this is the very method one uses to domesticate any old animal. "Teaching" a dog means nothing more than “making it obedient” to the will of its master, humanizing it. Which is a form of canine degeneration, just like the frequent dehumanization of a man into a dog—I refer to Osvaldo Dragún’s theatrical work.

The social logic of it is not much different. Whoever has power is the one who defines what a particular word means. Social obedience is implicit. In this sense, there are key words that have been colonized in our culture, words like democracy, freedom, justice, patriot, development, civilization, barbarism, etc. If we observe the definition of each one of these words derived from the same power—the same master—we will see that it is only by dint of a violent, colonizing and monopolistic “learning” that the term is applied to a particular case and not to another one, to one appearance and not to another, to one flag and not another—and almost always with the compelling force of the obvious. It is this logic alone that dominates the discourse and headlines of daily newspapers the world over. Even the loser, who receives the semiotic stigma, must use this language, these ideological tools to defend (timidly) any position that differs from the official, established one.

What we are experiencing at present is a profound crisis that naturally derives from a radical change in system—structural and mental: from a system of representative obedience to a system of progressive democracy.

It is not by accident that this current reaction against the disobedience of peoples would take the form of a renaissance of religious authoritarianism, in the East as much as in the West. Here we might say, like Pi i Margall in 1853, that "revolution is peace and reaction is war." The difference in our time is rooted in the fact that both revolution and reaction are invisible; they are camouflaged by the chaos of events, by the messianic and apocalyptic discourses, disguised in the old reading codes inherited from the Modern Era.

Now, how does one sustain this reaction against radical democratization, which is the invisible and perhaps inevitable revolution? We might continue observing that one form of attack against this democratization is for the reaction itself to kidnap the very idea of "democracy." But now let's mention just a few of the least abstract symptoms.

At the center of the "developed world," the most important television and radio networks repeat tiresomely the idea that "we are at war" and that "we must confront an enemy that wants to destroy us." The evil desire of minority groups—minority but growing—is unquestionable. The objective, our destruction, is infinitely improbable; except, that is, for the assistance offered by self-betrayal, which consists in copying all of the defects of the enemy one pretends to combat. Not coincidentally, the same discourse is repeated among Muslim peoples—without even beginning to consider anyone outside this simple dichotomy, product of another typical creation of the powers in conflict: the creation of false dilemmas.

In the most recent war, irrigated as always with copious innocent blood, we witnessed the repetition of the old model that is repeated every day and ceaselessly in so many corners of the world. A colonel, speaking from we know not which front, declared to a television channel of the Civilized World, dramatically: "It is on this road where the future of humanity will be decided; it is here where the 'clash of civilizations' is unfolding." Throughout that day, as with all the previous days and all the days after, the words and ideas repeated over and over again were: enemy, war, danger, imminent, civilization and barbarism, etc. To raise doubts about this would be like denying the Holy Trinity before the Holy Inquisition or, even worse, questioning the virtues of money before Calvin, God's chosen one. Because it is enough for one fanatic to call another fanatic "barbaric" or "infidel" to get others to agree that he needs to be killed. The final result is that it is rare for one of these barbaric people not to die by their own choice; most of those eliminated by the virtue of holy wars are innocents who would never choose to die. As in the time of Herod, the threat of the individual is eliminated by assassinating his entire generation—without ever achieving the objective, of course.

There is no choice: "it is necessary to win this war." But it turns out that this war will produce no victors, only losers: peoples who do not trade in human flesh. The strangest thing is that "on this side" the ones who favor every possible war are the most radical Christians, when it was none other than Christ who opposed, in word and deed, all forms of violence, even when he could have crushed with the mere wave of his hand the entire Roman Empire—the center of civilization at the time—and his torturers as well. If the "religious leaders" of today had a miniscule portion of the infinite power of Jesus, they would invest it in winning their unfinished wars. Obviously if huge Christian sects, in an historic act of benediction and justification for the insatiable accumulation of wealth, have been able to pass an army of camels through the eye of that particular needle, how could the difficult precept of turning the other cheek present a problem? Not only is the other cheek not offered—which is only human, even though it's not very Christian—instead the most advanced forms of violence are brought to bear on distant nations in the name of Right, Justice, Peace and Freedom—and of Christian values. And even though among them there is no recourse to the private relief of Catholic confession, they often practice it anyway after a bombardment of scores of innocents: "we are so sorry…"

On another television program, a report showed Muslim fanatics sermonizing the masses, calling upon them to combat the Western enemy. The journalists asked professors and analysts "how is a Muslim fanatic created?" To which each specialist attempted to give a response by referring to the wickedness of these terrible people and other metaphysical arguments that, despite being useless for explaining something rationally, are quite useful for feeding the fear and desire for combat of their faithful viewers. It never occurs to them to consider the obvious: a Muslim fanatic is created in exactly the same way that a Christian fanatic is created, or a Jewish fanatic: believing themselves to be in possession of the absolute truth, the best morality and law and, above all, to be executors of the will of God—violence willing. To prove this one has only to take a look at the various holocausts that humanity has promoted in its brief history: none of them has lacked for Noble Purposes; almost all were committed with pride by the privileged sons of God.

If one is a true believer one should start by not doubting the sacred text that serves as the foundation of the doctrine or religion. This, which seems logical, becomes tragic when a minority demands from the rest of the nation the same attitude of blind obedience, usurping God's role in representing God. What operates here is a transference of faith in the sacred texts to faith in the political texts. The King's minister becomes the Prime Minister and the King ceases to govern. In most of the mass media we are not asked to think; we are asked to believe. It is the advertising dynamic that shapes consumers with discourses based on simplification and obviousness. Everything is organized in order to convince us of something or to ratify our faith in a group, in a system, in a party. All in the guise of tolerance and diversity, of discussion and debate, where typically a grey representative of the contrarian position is invited to the table in order to humiliate or mock him. The committed journalist, like the politician, is a pastor who directs himself to an audience accustomed to hearing unquestionable sermons and theological opinions as if they were the word of God himself.

These observations are merely a beginning, because we would have to be very naïve indeed if we were to ignore the calculus of material interests on the part of the powerful, who—at least so far—have always decided, thumb up or thumb down, the fate of the innocent masses. Which is demonstrated by simply observing that the hundreds and thousands of innocent victims, aside from the occasional apology for mistakes made, are never the focus of the analysis about the wars and the permanent state of psychological, ideological and spiritual tension. (As an aside, I think it would be necessary to develop a scientific investigation regarding the heart rate of the viewers before and after witnessing an hour of these "informational" programs—or whatever you want to call them, since, in reality, the most informative part of these programs is the advertisements; the informational programming itself is propaganda, from the very moment in which they reproduce the colonized language.)

Dialogue has been cut off and the positions have polarized, poisoned by the hatred distilled by the big media, instruments of traditional power. "They are the incarnation of Evil"; "Our values are superior and therefore we have the right to exterminate them." "The fate of humanity depends upon our success." Etcetera. In order for success to be possible we must first guarantee the obedience of our fellow citizens. But it remains to be asked whether "success in the war" is really the main objective or instead a mere means, ever deferrable, for maintaining the obedience of one's own people, a people that was threatening to become independent and develop new forms of mutual understanding with other peoples. For all of this, propaganda, which is the propagation of hate, is indispensable. The beneficiaries are a minority; the majority simply obeys with passion and fanaticism: it is the culture of hate that sickens us day after day. But the culture of hate is not the metaphysical origin of Evil; it is little more than an instrument of other interests. Because if hatred is a sentiment that can be democratized, in contrast private interests to date have been the property of an elite. Until Humanity understands that the wellbeing of the other does me no harm but quite the opposite: if the other does not hate, if the other is not oppressed by me, then I will also benefit from the other's society. But one will have a heck of a time explaining this to the oppressor or to the oppressed; they will quickly come to an agreement to feed off of that perverse circle that keeps us from evolving together as Humanity.

Humanity will resist, as it has always resisted the most important changes in history. Resistance will not come from millions of innocents, for whom the benefits of historical progress will never arrive. For them is reserved the same old story: pain, torture and anonymous death that could have been avoided, at least in part, if the culture of hate had been replaced by the mutual comprehension that one day will be inevitable: the other is not necessarily an enemy that I must exterminate by poisoning my own brothers; what is to the benefit of the other will be to my benefit also.

This principle was Jesus's conscience, a conscience that was later corrupted by centuries of religious fanaticism, the most anti-Christian Gospel imaginable. And the same could be said of other religions.

In 1866 Juan Montalvo testified to his own bitterness: "The most civilized peoples, those whose intelligence has taken flight to the heavens and whose practices are guided by morality, do not renounce war: their breasts are ever burning, their zealous heart leaps with the impulse for extermination." And later: "The peace of Europe is not the peace of Jesus Christ, no: the peace of Europe is the peace of France and England, lack of confidence, mutual fear, threat; the one has armies sufficient to dominate the world, and only for that believes in peace; the other extends itself over the seas, controls every strait, rules the most important fortresses on earth, and only for that believes in peace."

If knowledge—or ignorance—is demonstrated by speaking, wisdom is the superior state in which a man or a woman learns to listen. As Eduardo Galeano rightly recommended to the powerful of the world, the ruler's job should be to listen more and speak less. Although only a rhetorical recommendation—in the sense that it is useless to give advice to those who will not listen—this remains an irrefutable principle for any democrat. But the discourses of the mass media and of the states, designed for creating soldiers, are only concerned with disciplining according to their own rules. Their struggle is the consolidation of ideological meaning in a colonized language divorced from the everyday reality of the speaker: their language is terribly creative of a terrible reality, almost always through abuse of the paradox and the oxymoron—as one might view the very notion of "communication media." It is the autistic symptom of our societies that day after day they sink further into the culture of hate. It is information and it is deformation.

In many previous essays, I have departed from and arrived at two presuppositions that seem contradictory. The first: it is not true that history never repeats itself; it always repeats itself; it is only appearances that are not repeated. The second precept, at least four hundred years old: history progresses. That is to say, humanity learns from past experience and in the process overcomes itself. Both human realities have always battled each other. If the human race remembered better and were less hypocritical, if it had greater awareness of its importance and were more rebellious against its false impotence, if instead of accepting the artificial fatalism of Clash of Civilizations it were to recognize the urgency of a Dialogue of Cultures, this battle would not sow the fields with corpses and nations with hate. The process of history, from its economic roots, is determined by and cannot be contradictory to the interests of humanity. What remains to be known is only how and when. If we accompany it with the new awareness demanded by posterity, we will not only advance a perhaps inevitable process; above all we will avoid more pain and the spilling of blood and death that has tinged the world hate-red in this greatest crisis of history.

(2006)

Rock Democracies, Paper Freedoms, Scissors Securities

In 1998, contradicting the postmodernist wave, we developed in *Crítica de la pasión pura* (*Critique of Pure Passion*) the idea of morality as a form of collective conscience. In the same way that James Lovelock understood Gaia—Planet Earth—as one living body, we could also understand Humanity as one conscience in development, with some common and basic values that transcend cultural differences.

These values are based, overwhelmingly, on the renunciation of the individual in favor of the group, on the conscience that supersedes the more primitive precept of the survival of the fittest, as mere individuals in competition. That is how the representation of the hero and of any other positive figure emerges throughout history.

The problem, the betrayal, is produced when these values become myths at the service of classes and sects in power. The worst thing that can happen to freedom is for it to be turned into a statue. The "conflicts of interests," normally presented as natural, from a broader perspective would represent a pathology. A culture that supports and legitimizes this betrayal of the conscience of the species should be seen—to use the same metaphor—as a self-destructive phobia of that *species conscience*.

Probably a form of radical democracy will be the next step humanity is ready to take. How will we know when this step is being produced? We need signs.

One strong sign will be when the administration of meaning ceases to lie in the hands of elites, especially of political elites. Representative democracy represents what is reactionary about our times. But direct democracy will not come about through any brusque revolution, led by individuals, since it is, by definition, a cultural process where the majority begins to claim and share social power. When this occurs, the parliaments of the world will be what the royals of England are today: an onerous adornment from the past, an illusion of continuity.

Every time "public opinion" changes suddenly after an official speech, after an electoral campaign, after a bombardment of advertising—power that always flows from the money of a minority —we must understand that that next step remains far from being consolidated. When publics become independent of the speeches, when the speeches and social narrations no longer depend on the powerful minorities, we will be able to think about certain advance toward direct democracy.

Let's look briefly at this problematic of the struggle over meaning.

There are words with scarce social interest and others that are disputed treasure, territory claimed by different antagonistic groups. In the first category we can recognize words like *umbrella*, *glycemia*, *fame*, *hurricane*, *nice*, *anxiety*, etc. In the second category we find terms like *freedom*, *democracy* and *justice* (we will call these ideolexicons). *Reality* and *normal* are also highly disputed terms, but generally they are restricted to philosophical speculation. Unless they are instruments—like the definition of *normal*—they are not direct objectives of social power.

The eternal struggle for social power creates a partisan culture made visible by the so-called political parties. In general, it is these same parties that make possible the continuity of a particular social power by creating the illusion of a possible change. Because of this culture, we tend to adopt a position with respect to each social problem instead of a dispassionate analysis of it. Ideological loyalty or self-love should not be involved in these cases, but we cannot deny that they are fundamental pieces of the dialectical dispute and they weigh on us all.

All conflict is established in a present time but recurs obsessively to a prestigious, consolidated past. Recurring to that same history, each antagonistic group, whether in Mexico or in the United States, will seek to conquer the semantic field with different narrations, each one of which will have as a requirement the *unity* and *continuity* of that narrative thread. Rarely do the groups in dispute prove something; generally, they *narrate*. Like in a traditional novel, the narration does not depend so much on facts external to the story as on the internal coherence and verisimilitude possessed by that narration. For that reason, when one of the actors in the dispute—a congressional representative, a president—recognizes an error, this becomes a greater crack in the story than if reality contradicted him every day. Why? Because the imagination is stronger than reality and the latter, generally speaking, cannot be observed except through a discourse, a *narration*.

The difference lies in which interests are moved by each narration. A slave receiving lashes of the whip and giving thanks for the favor received is not the same as another version of the facts that questions that concept of *justice*. Perhaps objectivity does not exist, but the presumption of reality and, therefore, of a possible truth will always exist.

One of the more common methods used to administer or dispute the meaning of each term, of each concept, is *semantic association*. It is the same resource that allows advertising to freely associate a shaving cream with economic success or an automotive lubricant with sexual success.

When the value of racial integration found itself in dispute in the social discourse of the 1950s and 1960s in the United States, various groups of southern whites marched through the streets carrying placards that declared: *Race mixing is communism* (*Time*, August 24, 1959). The same placard in Poland would have been a declaration in favor of racial integration, but in the times of McCarthy it meant quite the contrary: the word *communism* had been consolidated as a negative ideolect. The meaning was not disputed. Anything that might be associated with that demon was condemned to death or at least to failure.

Recent history tells us that that association failed, at least in the collective narration about the value of "racial integration." So much so that today the banner of *diversity* is used as an inarguable axiom. Which is why the new racists must integrate to their own purposes narratives of *diversity* as a positive value in order to develop a new narration against immigrants.

In other cases the mechanism is similar. Recently, a U.S. legislator, criticized for calling Miami "third world," declared that he is *in favor of diversity* as long as *a single language and a single culture is imposed on the entire country*, (*World Net Daily*, December 13) and there are no "extensive ethnic neighborhoods where English is not spoken and that are controlled by foreign cultures." (*Diario de las Américas*, November 11)

All hegemonic power needs a moral legitimation and this is achieved by constructing a narration that integrates those *ideolexicons* that are not in dispute. When Hernán Cortés or Pizarro cut off hands and heads they did it in the name of divine justice and by order of God. Incipiently the idea of *liberation* began to emerge. The messianic powers of the moment understood that by imposing their own religion and their own culture, almost always by force, they were liberating the primitive Americans from idolatry.

Today the ideolexicon *democracy* has been imposed in such a way that it is even used to name authoritarian and theocratic systems. Minority groups that decide every day the difference between life and death for thousands of people, if indeed in private they don't devalue the old argument of salvation and divine justice, tend to prefer in public the less problematic banner of *democracy* and *freedom*. Both ideolexicons are so positive that their imposition is justified even if it is intravenously.

Because they imposed a culture by force the Spanish conquistadors are remembered as barbaric. Those who do the same today are motivated, this time for sure, by good reasons: democracy, freedom —*our values*, which are always the best. But just as the heroes of yesterday are today's barbarians, the heroes of today will be the barbarians of tomorrow.

If morality and its most basic extracts represent the *collective conscience* of the species, it is probable that direct democracy will come to signify a form of *collective thought*. Paradoxically, collective thinking is incompatible with uniform thinking. This for reasons noted previously: uniform thinking can be the result of a sectarian interest, a class interest, a national interest. In contrast, collective thinking is perfected in the diversity of all possibilities, acting in benefit of Humanity and not on behalf of minorities in conflict.

In a similar scenario, it is not difficult to imagine a new era with fewer sectarian conflicts and absurd wars that only benefit seven powerful riders, while entire nations die, fanatically or unwilling, in the name of order, freedom and justice.

(2004)

Patriarchy with a Woman's Face

The same day that Joe Biden is selected as candidate for the vice presidency by the Democratic Party of 2008, the campaign of John McCain reproduced several videos of Hillary Clinton sharply attacking Obama. Probably these ads were designed with a selection of Clinton in mind instead of Biden. But even though this expectation was not met, Republican Party strategists must have thought that such critical work should not be thrown away and chose to put it on the air anyway. Immediately afterward, McCain's advertising called explicitly for Clinton's sad supporters to vote for the Republicans, just as the old democratic candidate Joe Lieberman does now, allying himself with his ex-rival from the 2000 elections, George Bush, in support of McCain with the argument for the latter's greater experience.

Shortly before the Republican candidate was to announce his selection for VP, a radio station called me to talk about this process. At that moment there were three names in play, all men, but considering the electoral market it was my opinion that McCain's vice presidential candidate would be a woman. Since then we have not stopped hearing women's groups and Sarah Palin appeal to women's consciousness in order to gain power. If it is indeed true that there is still a long way to go to eliminate the arbitrary inequalities of power, perhaps one particular woman is not the best substitute for women in general.

There are still feminists today who take pride in Margaret Thatcher for having been a woman of steel in power in one of the old empires, even though women who ordered their black slaves whipped had already been abundant for centuries. It remains paradoxical that it was precisely Ronald Reagan and Margaret Thatcher who put the brakes on the progressive movements, among them the feminists, that appeared in the 1960s and which represented a rebellion of minority groups and of the oppressed (although in reality this was only a consequence of a long historical process initiated, in my view, in the 15th century).

All of that, which was barely the visible and ambiguous face of a deeper historical change, was reversed by the conservative wave that, in my opinion, will be coming to an end in the next decade but which can be slowed down in its movement, depending on the success or failure of some political changes around the world, especially in the United States. In whatever form, even if postponed, inexorable generational change will not depend on any political party. But right now possibility matters.

Sarah Palin is recognized as one of the most conservative among the conservative politicians. She is associated, for example, with "pro-life" groups. The latest slogan prays "Pro-Life, Pro-Palin," in the assumed ideolexicon suggesting that others are not in favor of life. This defender of life supports unconditionally the war in Iraq and anywhere else it might be necessary. She is a member of the powerful National Rifle Association. She can be seen in photographs posing together with her children, smiling as beautifully as Diana, with a rifle in hand next to a moose she brought down herself, lying in a pool of blood in the snow. It is likely that the fondness for hunting and weapons on the part of the governor of Alaska and "pro-life" conservatives is not for fun or for sport, but out of necessity.

Significantly, the major stir that Sarah Palin has produced in recent days came with revelations of the pregnancy out of wedlock of one of her daughters. The scandal of the revelation, not of the pregnancy, is attributed to leftist press like the New York Times. Nonetheless, the fact must be of interest to conservatives, who are always concerned about the sexual life of sinners. However, various groups of conservative women, among them Jane Swift, the ex-governor of Massachusetts, declared that all of the criticisms of Palin are sexist, since Palin is a woman. It is not sexist that, according to Hillary Clinton, it is acceptable to McCain and the conservatives that a woman receives a lower salary for the same work as a man because women are less educated than men.

From the conservative wing of the U.S. political spectrum, to which Palin belongs, have come theories that can in no way be called progressive and where being feminist is an insult as serious as being gay, liberal or an intellectual. In fact the intellectuals of this ideological region hate intellectuals in general and their books, and with a deep psychological need to police they dedicate themselves to making black lists of people, almost always colleagues, who they subsequently call "dangerous" or "stupid," as if a stupid intellectual could be dangerous at the same time, the way a stupid president can be. From their pens have come impoverished but well publicized theories, like the theories of the return of patriarchy according to which the fact that a woman complies with the fixed role of stay-at-home mother produces families with many children, and consequently sustains the hegemony of an empire. Toward this end they cite not only the decline of the Roman Empire but the high birth rate of conservative families in the southern states in comparison with the low birth rate of liberal families in the north (e.g., Phillip Longman).

One cannot say that this is a campaign filled with rhetoric because it does not even amount to that much. Everything is reduced to the repetition of six or seven clichés whenever possible and even whenever irrelevant. One of the preferred clichés consists in emphasizing the experience of the candidate and their family values. Question: "What is the central idea of your candidate?" Answer (eyes fixed on the camera, face impassive): "The other candidate does not have the necessary experience."

Experience is the other supreme virtue that is attributed to Sarah Palin when it is suggested that she has none. Almost as much as George Bush, who has had more than enough experience even before the beginning of his career and who has been so unjustly criticized and attacked by Democrats and avoided by his own party but recognized by the conservatives for his family values and for his respect for his self-sacrificing wife. A man who from the beginning stood out not only for his incredibly broad political experience but also for his intelligence and his culture, although to these last two faculties one might add the generous virtue of discretion.

In summation and in their own words, conservatives are defenders of the values of the family. That is, authority proceeds from the father and fathers have the biblical right to define what is a family and what are its values. They are respectful and do not invade the private life of gays and lesbians as long as gays and lesbians do not attempt to obtain the same civil rights as decent people. The traditional role of the woman has been established by tradition and questioning that is part of the corruption and lack of values, all characteristics of the "bitter leftists," liberals, and feminists.

Nevertheless, according to the polls, millions of women who previously supported Hillary Clinton have gone over to the Republican side. The electoral market, like on other occasions, is nourished by the contradictions of its consumers: those women who passionately defend in the media and in the cafes their support for a woman as a strategic advantage for the feminist movement without caring that that woman represents the exact opposite, may signify for the more sophisticated a demonstration of false consciousness, of complete manipulation. Something along the lines of women's liberation through the consolidation of patriarchy, or the feminization of feminism.

We hope, in this context, that such brilliant masters of political chess will continue then to promise more freedom, democracy, and justice, and to always speak the truth, the whole truth, and nothing but the truth.

(2008)

White x black = black

The central theme of the debates in the Democratic Party primaries in the US is an interesting case and, whatever the result, it will represent only a relative change. This is no surprise, for those who see it from an historical perspective.

Without a doubt, a victory by Hillary Clinton will not be as significant as a victory by Obama. They are not separated so much by gender or race as by a generational gap. One represents a hegemonic past and the other one represents a slightly more critical and disillusioned youth. A generation, I believe, that will implement important changes in the coming decades.

Essentially, what has still not changed radically are the old race and gender issues. The main and fundamental theme of the debates has been exactly that: gender or race, even when we are assured the contrary is the case. It is significant that in the middle of an economic crisis and fears of a recession, the most heated discussions are not on the economy but on gender and race. In the economic super-power that has dominated or influenced the life of almost every country on the planet with its economic might, the economy has seldom been the central issue the way it tends to be in Latin American countries. At the same time, I understand that the general lack of interest in politics is peculiar to the population of a world's political power.

Whenever there is a fiscal deficit, a fall in the GDP, or an increasingly weak dollar, the most conservative elements in the US political establishment always bring out their favorite scare tactics: the foreign threat, the war on terror, the defense of the family, the denial of civil rights to same sex couples and in general terms, the defense of "values," i.e., moral values according to their own interpretations and expediencies.

But now the most recent opinion polls show that the economy is very quickly becoming one of the main issues that concern the electorate. This happens whenever the economic machinery approaches a recession. Nevertheless, the presidential candidates are afraid to distance themselves too much from the usual conservative rhetoric. Perhaps Obama has gone a little further on this score by criticizing the abuse of religion and certain kinds of "patriotism," while Hillary has revived the brief but very effective slogan used by her husband in 1992, in the middle of the recession created by president George H.W. Bush, which carried Bill Clinton to victory: "It's the economy, stupid." Its easy accessibility was due to a simplicity that even the McDonald's generation can understand.

Hillary Clinton is the daughter of a man and a woman but, in spite of what psychoanalysis might say, everyone sees her as a woman and that's it. Barack Obama is the son of a white woman and a black man, but he is black, and that's it. All this can be deduced from the language used by both the mass media and the electorate. No one has observed anything so obvious as the fact that he could be viewed to be just as white as he is black, if we accept these arbitrary categories. This represents the same difficulty with seeing the mixture of cultures in the famous "melting pot": the elements are interspersed, but never combine together. From the melting of copper and tin we do not obtain bronze, but copper and tin. One is black or one is white. One is Hispanic or one is Asian.

The one who has suffered is John Edwards, a talented white man who escaped poverty and seems not to have forgotten what it is like, but who offers nothing politically correct to attract voters. He is not even ugly or ill-mannered, factors which tend to produce sympathy or compassion in the general public.

But words can—and in politics, almost always do—create a conflicting reality: Hillary Clinton said a few days ago, in South Carolina, that she loved the primaries because the choice was between nominating an African-American or a woman and neither of them was going to lose even one vote because of who they are. Here the word "sex" is studiously avoided: "I love these primaries because it looks like we are going to nominate an African-American man or a woman and they aren't going to lose any vote because of their race or gender." This is why Obama speaks to women and Clinton to African-Americans. This is also why in South Carolina nearly 80% of the black population and only 20%

of whites voted for Obama. This is why Florida and California, the two states with the largest Hispanic populations, refused to support Obama, who is a member of another minority.

And so, while it has become customary to scorn what is labeled as "politically correct," no one seems to want to stop being just that. The debates of the 2008 elections remind me of McDonald's Happy Meal boxes. Such abundance of joy, happiness and happy smiles are not necessarily a sign of health. The head of the State Department in the world's only super-power is a black woman. For years, an African-American woman has had more influence on a multitude of countries than millions of white men. Nevertheless, the black population of the United States—like that of many Latin American countries—is still not proportionally represented among the upper classes, the universities and the legislatures, whereas, they are significantly over-represented in the poorest neighborhoods and the prisons where they fight to the death with Hispanics over hegemony of this dubious kingdom.

(2008)

THE FAULT IS OF THE POOR

In 1758, the Governor of South Carolina, James Glen, acknowledged in a letter to his successor: "It has always been the policy of this government to create an aversion in them to Indians to Negroes."

In previous generations, racism had not reached a sufficient level of hatred to prevent Indians, blacks, and poor whites from joining together for work, intimacy and, above all, to rebel against the power of the powerful.

The fault of violence was of the poor.

Today, two of the world's most lucrative businesses are drug trafficking and arms sales.

Because drug production is in poor countries and consumption in rich countries, the blame for violence is on the producers, that is, on the poor.

Because the production of weapons is in rich countries and consumption in poor countries, the fault of the violence is on consumers, that is, the poor.

When the economy in rich countries thrives, the poor are the only ones to blame for their own poverty, as if the world were flat and everyone had the same opportunities.

When the economy in rich countries stagnates, or recedes, then the poor are to blame for the fact that others do not have jobs. Especially if they are poor immigrants.

The fault is always of the poor.

The Statue of Liberty of New York received millions of immigrants (Europeans), without visas or passports, with the verses:

"Give me your tired, your poor,
Your huddled masses yearning to breathe free,
The wretched refuse of your teeming shore.
Send these, the homeless, tempest-tossed to me"

However, now, according to the laws in rich countries, if someone is rich, a visa or a permanent residence is almost guaranteed. If someone is poor and his flag is *work*, he or she will be automatically blocked from entering rich countries.

In fact, the single word "working" at any consulate in the world is the first key that turns on all the alarms and closes the doors to an honest worker.

Because a world obsessed with growth, where capital produces more capital, does not believe that labor can produce more labor.

Because money is freer than human beings and a human being without money is not free but a slave.

To justify this global apartheid, we no longer resort to the concept of race but that of nations, and we confuse legality with legitimacy, as if the laws were not the expression of the convenciences of the power of the day, as if the laws were not often elegant ways to legalize the corruption of power.

Even the best laws are often unfair, especially with those who are not in power. As an example, the French novelist Anatole France made a remark a hundred years ago: "In its majestic equality, the law forbids rich and poor alike to sleep under bridges, beg in the streets and steal loaves of bread."

Because the fault is always of the poor.

(2017)

The Pandemic of Consumerism

Periods of global warming are not in and of themselves a human invention. But humans have invented ways of turning a natural cycle into an abnormality whose severity can exceed the tragedy of an atomic bomb, or even of several. Nonetheless, we don't see the explosion because we're living inside of it, because it seems like an unremediable quirk of nature to which we must all resign ourselves.

The world's governments are too busy trying to save humanity from the "great crisis" —the economic crisis— by stimulating the same consumption that is leading us to unmitigated disaster. If the level of global destruction has not yet reached the dreaded status of full-blown catastrophe, it is only because consumerism has not yet reached its supposedly desired levels.

In this collective delirium, development is confused with consumerism, waste with success, and growth with feeding frenzy. The pandemic is considered a sign of good health. Its "success" has been so overwhelming that there is no ideology or political system in the world that is not bent upon reproducing and multiplying it.

New technologies could help to reduce carbon dioxide emissions, but it is unlikely that this would be sufficient in a world that is just at the beginning of its capacity to consume, to squander, and to destroy. Attempting to reduce environmental pollution without reducing consumerism is like combatting drug trafficking without reducing the drug addiction.

Wasteful and irrational consumerism has no limits; it has not prevented the death of millions of children from hunger, but it has endangered the existence of the entire biosphere. If "successful" consumerism is not replaced by the forgotten values of austerity, soon we will have to choose between war and misery, hunger and epidemics.

It is in the hands of governments and in the hands of each of us to either organize the salvation or accelerate the destruction of our world. The Climate Change Conference in Copenhagen is a new opportunity to prevent the greatest calamity humanity has ever faced. Let us not have another opportunity missed, because we certainly do not have all the time in the world.

(2009)

IV. Religion and other excuses

THE SLOW SUICIDE OF THE WEST

The West appears, suddenly, devoid of its greatest virtues, constructed century after century, preoccupied now only with reproducing its own defects and with copying the defects of others, such as authoritarianism and the preemptive persecution of innocents. Virtues like tolerance and self-criticism have never been a weakness, as some now pretend, but quite the opposite: it was because of these that progress, both ethical and material, was possible. Both the greatest hope and the greatest danger for the West can be found at the heart of its own culture. Those of us who hold neither "Rage" nor "Pride" for any race or culture feel nostalgia for times gone by, times that were never especially good, but were not so bad either.

Currently, some celebrities from back in the 20th century, demonstrating an irreversible decline into senility, have taken to propagating the famous ideology of the "clash of civilizations"—which was already plenty vulgar all by itself—basing their reasoning on their own conclusions, in the best style of classical theology. Such is the a priori and 19th century assertion that

"Western culture is superior to all others." And, as if that were not enough, that it is a moral obligation to go around repeating it.

From this perspective of Western Superiority, the quite famous Italian journalist Oriana Fallaci wrote, recently, brilliant observations such as the following: "If in some countries the women are so stupid as to accept the *chador* and even the veil, so much the worse for them. (…) And if their husbands are so idiotic as to not drink wine or beer, idem." Wow, that is what I call intellectual rigor. "How disgusting!"—she continued, first in the *Corriere della Sera* and later in her best seller *The Rage and the Pride* (Rizzoli International, 2002), referring to the Africans who had urinated in a plaza in Italy— "They piss for a long time these sons of Allah! A race of hypocrites." "Even if they were absolutely innocent, even if there were not one among them who wished to destroy the Tower of Pisa or the Tower of Giotto, not one who wished to make me wear the *chador*, not one who wished to burn me on the bonfires of a new Inquisition, their presence alarms me. It makes me uneasy." Summing up: even if these blacks were completely innocent, their presence makes her uneasy anyway. For Fallaci, this is not racism; it is "cold, lucid, rational rage." And, if that were not enough, she offers another ingenious observation with reference to immigrants in general: "And besides, there is something else I don't understand. If they are really so poor, who gives them the money for the trip on the planes or boats that bring them to Italy? Might Osama bin Laden be paying their way, at least in part?" Poor Galileo, poor Camus, poor Simone de Beauvoir, poor Michel Foucault.

Incidentally, we should remember that, even though the lady writes without understanding—she said it herself—these words ended up in a book that has sold a half million copies, a book with no shortage of reasoning and common sense, as when she asserts "I am an atheist, thank God." Nor does it lack in historical curiosities like the following: "How does one accept polygamy and the principle that women should not allow photographs to be taken of them? Because this is also in the Q'uran," which means that in the 7th century Arabs were extremely advanced in the area of optics. Nor is the book lacking in repeated doses of humor, as with these weighty arguments: "And, besides, let's admit it: our cathedrals are more beautiful than the mosques and synagogues, yes or no? Protestant churches are also more beautiful." As Atilio says, she has the Shine of Brigitte Bardot. As if what we really needed was to get wrapped up in a discussion of which is more beautiful, the Tower of Pisa or the Taj Mahal. And once again that European tolerance: "I am telling you that, precisely because it has been well defined for centuries, our cultural identity cannot support a wave of immigration composed of people who, in one form or another, want to change our way of life. Our values. I am telling you that among us there is no room for muezzins, for minarets, for false abstinence, for their screwed up medieval ways, for their damned chador. And if there were, I would not give it to them." And finally, concluding with a warning to her editor: "I warn you: do not ask me for anything else ever again. Least of all that I participate in vain polemics. What I needed to say I have said. My rage and pride have demanded it of me." Something which had already been clear to us from the beginning and, as it happens, denies us one of the basic elements of both democracy and tolerance, dating to ancient Greece: polemics and the right to respond—the competition of arguments instead of insults.

But I do not possess a name as famous as Fallaci—a fame well-deserved, we have no reason to doubt—and so I cannot settle for insults. Since I am native to an under-developed country and am not even as famous as Maradona, I have no other choice than to take recourse to the ancient custom of using arguments.

Let's see. The very expression "Western culture" is just as mistaken as the terms "Eastern culture" or "Islamic culture," because each one of them is made up of a diverse and often contradictory collection of other "cultures." One need only think of the fact that within "Western culture" one can fit not only countries as different as the United States and Cuba, but also irreconcilable historical periods within the same geographic region, such as tiny Europe and the even tinier Germany, where Goethe and Adolf Hitler, Bach and the skin-heads, have all walked the earth. On the other hand, let's not forget also that Hitler and the Ku Klux Klan (in the name of Christ and the White Race), Stalin (in the name of Reason and atheism), Pinochet (in the name of Democracy and Liberty), and Mussolini (in his own name), were typical recent products and representatives of the self-proclaimed "Western culture." What is more Western than democracy and concentration camps? What could be more Western that the Universal Declaration of Human Rights and the dictatorships in Spain and Latin America, bloody and degenerate beyond the imagination? What is more Western than Christianity, which cured, saved and assassinated thanks to the Holy Office? What is more Western than the modern military academies or the ancient monasteries where the art of torture was taught, with the most refined sadism, and by the initiative of Pope Innocent IV and based on Roman Law? Or did Marco Polo bring all of that back from the Middle East? What could be more Western than the atomic bomb and the millions of dead and disappeared under the fascist, communist and, even, "democratic" regimes? What more Western than the military invasions and suppression of entire peoples under the so-called "preemptive bombings"?

All of this is the dark side of the West and there is no guarantee that we have escaped any of it, simply because we haven't been able to communicate with our neighbors, who have been there for more than 1400 years, with the only difference that now the world has been globalized (the West has globalized it) and the neighbors possess the main source of energy that moves the world's economy—at least for the moment—in addition to the same hatred and the same rancor as Oriana Fallaci. Let's not forget that the Spanish Inquisition, more of a state-run affair than the others, originated from hostility toward the Moors and Jews and did not end with the Progress and Salvation of Spain but with the burning of thousands of human beings.

Nevertheless, the West also represents Democracy, Freedom, Human Rights and the struggle for women's rights. At least the effort to attain them, and the most that humanity has achieved so far. And what has always been the basis of those four pillars, if not tolerance?

Fallaci would have us believe that "Western culture" is a unique and pure product, without the Other's participation. But if anything characterizes the West, it has been precisely the opposite: we are the result of countless cultures, beginning with the Hebrew culture (to say nothing of Amenophis IV) and continuing through almost all the rest: through the Caldeans, the Greeks, the Chinese, the Hindus, the southern Africans, the northern Africans and the rest of the cultures that today are uniformly described as "Islamic." Until recently, it would not have been necessary to remember that, while in Europe—in all of Europe—the Christian Church, in the name of Love, was persecuting, torturing and burning alive those who disagreed with the ecclesiastical authorities or committed the sin of engaging in some kind of research (or simply because they were single women, which is to say, witches), in the Islamic world the arts and sciences were being promoted, and not only those of the Islamic region but of the Chinese, Hindus, Jews and Greeks. And nor does this mean that butterflies flew and violins played everywhere. Between Baghdad and Córdoba the geographical distance was, at the time, almost astronomical.

But Oriana Fallacia not only denies the diverse and contradictory composition of any of the cultures in conflict, but also, in fact, refuses to acknowledge the Eastern counterpart as a culture at all. "It bothers me even to speak of two cultures," she writes. And then she dispatches the matter with an incredible display of historical ignorance: "Placing them on the same level, as if they were parallel realities, of equal weight and equal measure. Because behind our civilization are Homer, Socrates, Plato, Aristotle and Phidias, among many others. There is ancient Greece with its Parthenon and its discovery of Democracy. There is ancient Rome with its grandeur, its laws and its conception of the Law. With its sculpture, its literature and its architecture. Its palaces and its amphitheaters, its aqueducts, its bridges and its roads."

Is it really necessary to remind Fallaci that among all of that and all of us one finds the ancient Islamic Empire, without which everything would have burned—I am talking about the books and the people, not the Coliseum—thanks to centuries of ecclesiastical terrorism, quite European and quite Western? And with regard to the grandeur of Rome and "its conception of the Law" we will talk another day, because here there is indeed some black and white worth remembering. Let's also set aside for the moment Islamic literature and architecture, which have nothing to envy in Fallaci's Rome, as any half-way educated person knows.

Let's see, and lastly? "Lastly—writes Fallaci—there is science. A science that has discovered many illnesses and cures them. I am alive today, for the time being, thanks to our science, not Mohammed's. A science that has changed the face of this planet with electricity, the radio, the telephone, the television... Well then, let us ask now the fatal question: and behind the other culture, what is there?"

The fatal answer: behind our science one finds the Egyptians, the Caldeans, the Hindus, the Greeks, the Chinese, the Arabs, the Jews and the Africans. Or does Fallaci believe that everything arose through spontaneous generation in the last fifty years? She needs to be reminded that Pythagoras took his philosophy from Egypt and Caldea (Iraq)—including his famous mathematical formula, which we use not only in architecture but also in the proof of Einstein's Special Theory of Relativity—as did that other wise man and mathematician Thales. Both of them traveled through the Middle East with their minds more open than Fallaci's when she made the trip. The hypothetical-deductive method—the basis for scientific epistemology—originated among Egyptian priests (start with Klimovsky, please), zero and the extraction of square roots, as well as innumerable mathematical and astronomical discoveries, which we teach today in grade school, were born in India and Iraq; the alphabet was invented by the Phoenicians (ancient Lebanese), who were also responsible for the first form of globalization known to the world. The zero was not an invention of the Arabs, but of the Hindus, but it was the former who brought it to the West. By contrast, the advanced Roman Empire not only was unfamiliar with zero—without which it would be impossible to imagine modern mathematics and space travel—but in fact possessed an unwieldy system of counting and calculation that endured until the late Middle Ages. Through to the early Renaissance there were still businessmen who used the Roman system, refusing to exchange it for Arabic numerals, due to racial and religious prejudices, resulting in all kinds of mathematical errors and social disputes. Meanwhile, perhaps it is better to not even mention that the birth of the Modern Era began with European cultural contact—after long centuries of religious repression—first with Islamic culture and then with Greek culture. Or did anyone think that the rationalism of the Scholastics was a consequence of the practice of torture in the holy dungeons? In the early 12th century, the Englishman Adelard of Bath undertook an extensive voyage of study through the south of Europe, Syria and Palestine. Upon returning from his trip, Adelard introduced into under-developed England a paradigm that even today is upheld by famous scientists like Stephen Hawking: God had created Nature in such a way that it could be studied and explained without His intervention. (Behold the other pillar of the sciences, rejected historically by the Roman Church.) Indeed, Adelard reproached the thinkers of his time for having allowed themselves to be enthralled by the prestige of the authorities—beginning with Aristotle, clearly. Because of them he made use of the slogan "reason against authority," and insisted he be called "modernus." "I have learned from my Arab teachers to take reason as a guide—he wrote—but you only adhere to what authority says." A compatriot of Fallaci, Gerardo de Cremona, introduced to Europe the writings of the "Iraqi" astronomer and mathematician Al-Jwarizmi, inventor of algebra, of algorithms, of Arabic and decimal calculus; translated Ptolemy from the Arabic—since even the astronomical theory of an official Greek like Ptolemy could not be found in Christian Europe—as well as dozens of medical treatises, like those of Ibn Sina and Irani al-Razi, author of the first scientific treatise on smallpox and measles, for which today he might have been the object of some kind of persecution.

We could continue listing examples such as these, which the Italian journalist ignores, but that would require an entire book and is not the most important thing at the moment.

What is at stake today is not only protecting the West against the terrorists, home-grown and foreign, but—and perhaps above all—protecting the West from itself. The reproduction of any one of its most monstrous events would be enough to lose everything that has been attained to date with respect to Human Rights. Beginning with respect for diversity. And it is highly probable that such a thing could occur in the next ten years, if we do not react in time.

The seed is there and it only requires a little water. I have heard dozens of times the following expression: "the only good thing that Hitler did was kill all those Jews." Nothing more and nothing less. And I have not heard it from the mouth of any

Muslim—perhaps because I live in a country where they practically do not exist—nor even from anyone of Arab descent. I have heard it from neutral creoles and from people of European descent. Each time I hear it I need only respond in the following manner in order to silence my interlocutor: "What is your last name? Gutiérrez, Pauletti, Wilson, Marceau… Then, sir, you are not German, much less a pure Aryan. Which means that long before Hitler would have finished off the Jews he would have started by killing your grandparents and everyone else with a profile and skin color like yours." We run the same risk today: if we set about persecuting Arabs or Muslims we will not only be proving that we have learned nothing, but we will also wind up persecuting those like them: Bedouins, North Africans, Gypsies, Southern Spaniards, Spanish Jews, Latin American Jews, Central Americans, Southern Mexicans, Northern Mormons, Hawaiians, Chinese, Hindus, and so on.

Not long ago another Italian, Umberto Eco, summed up a sage piece of advice thusly: "We are a plural civilization because we permit mosques to be built in our countries, and we cannot renounce them simply because in Kabul they throw Christian propagandists in jail […] We believe that our culture is mature because it knows how to tolerate diversity, and members of our culture who don't tolerate it are barbarians."

As Freud and Jung used to say, that act which nobody would desire to commit is never the object of a prohibition; and as Boudrillard said, rights are established when they have been lost. The

Islamic terrorists have achieved what they wanted, twice over. The West appears, suddenly, devoid of its greatest virtues, constructed century after century, preoccupied now only with reproducing its own defects and with copying the defects of others, such as authoritarianism and the preemptive persecution of innocents. So much time imposing its culture on the other regions of the planet, to allow itself now to impose a morality that in its better moments was not even its own. Virtues like tolerance and self-criticism never represented its weakness, as some would now have it, but quite the opposite: only because of them was any kind of progress possible, whether ethical or material. Democracy and Science never developed out of the narcissistic reverence for its own culture but from critical opposition within it. And in this enterprise were engaged, until recently, not only the "damned intellectuals" but many activist and social resistance groups, like the bourgeoisie in the 18th century, the unions in the 20th century, investigative journalism until a short time ago, now replaced by propaganda in these miserable times of ours. Even the rapid destruction of privacy is another symptom of that moral colonization. Only instead of religious control we will be controlled by Military Security. The Big Brother who hears all and sees all will end up forcing upon us masks similar to those we see in the East, with the sole objective of not being recognized when we walk down the street or when we make love.

The struggle is not—nor should it be—between Easterners and Westerners; the struggle is between tolerance and imposition, between diversity and homogenization, between respect for the other and scorn and his annihilation. Writings like Fallaci's *The Rage and the Pride* are not a defense of Western culture but a cunning attack, an insulting broadside against the best of what Western culture has to offer. Proof of this is that it would be sufficient to swap the word Eastern for Western, and a geographical locale or two, in order to recognize the position of a Taliban fanatic. Those of us who have neither Rage nor Pride for any particular race or culture are nostalgic for times gone by, which were never especially good or especially bad.

A few years before I was in the United States and I saw there a beautiful mural in the United Nations building in New York, if I remember correctly, where men and women from distinct races and religions were visually represented—I think the composition was based on a somewhat arbitrary pyramid, but that is neither here nor there. Below, with gilded letters, one could read a commandment taught by Confucius in China and repeated for millennia by men and women throughout the East, until it came to constitute a Western principle: "Do unto others as you would have them do unto you." In English it sounds musical, and even those who do not know the language sense that it refers to a certain reciprocity between oneself and others. I do not understand why we should scratch that commandment from our walls—founding principle for any democracy and for the rule of law, founding principle for the best dreams of the West—simply because others have suddenly forgotten it. Or they have exchanged it for an ancient biblical principle that Christ took it upon himself to abolish: "an eye for an eye and a tooth for a tooth." Which at present translates as an inversion of the Confucian maxim, something like: do unto others everything that they have done to you—the well-known, endless story.

(2002)

The Privatization of God

In the 17th century, the mathematics genius Blaise Pascal wrote that men never do evil with greater pleasure than when they do it with religious conviction. This idea—from a deeply religious man—has taken a variety of different forms since. During the last century, the greatest crimes against humanity were promoted, with pride and passion, in the name of Progress, of Justice and of Freedom. In the name of Love, Puritans and moralists organized hatred, oppression and humiliation; in the name of Life, leaders and prophets spilled death over vast regions of the planet. Presently, God has come to be the main excuse for exercises in hate and death, hiding political ambitions, earthly and infernal interests behind sacred invocations. In this way, by reducing each tragedy on the planet to the millenarian and simplified tradition of the struggle between Good and Evil, of God against the Devil, hatred, violence and death are legitimated. There is no other way to explain how men and women are inclined to pray with fanatical pride and hypocritical humility, as if they were pure angels, models of morality, all the while hiding gunpowder in their clothing, or a check made out to death. And if the leaders are aware of the fraud, their subjects are no less responsible for being stupid, no less culpable for their criminal metaphysical convictions, in the name of God and Morality—when not in the name of a race, of a culture—and from a long tradition, recently on exhibit, custom-fit to the latest in hatred and ambition.

Yes, we can believe in the people. We can believe that they are capable of the most astounding creations—as will be one day their own liberation—and also of incommensurable stupidities, these latter always concealed by a complacent and self-interested discourse that manages to nullify criticism and any challenge to bad conscience. But, how did we come to such criminal negligence? Where does so much pride come from in a world where violence grows daily and more and more people claim to have heard the voice of God?

Political history demonstrates that a simplification is more powerful and better received by the vast majority of a society than is a problematization. For a politician or for a spiritual leader, for example, it is a show of weakness to admit that reality is complex. If one's adversary expunges from a problem all of its contradictions and presents it to the public as a struggle between Good and Evil, the adversary undoubtedly is more likely to triumph. In the final analysis, the primary lesson of our time is grounded in commercial advertising or in permissive submission: we elect and we buy that which solves our problems for us, quickly and cheaply, even though the problem might be created by the solution, and even though the problem might continue to be real while the solution is never more than virtual. Nonetheless, a simplification does not eliminate the complexity of the problem in question, but rather, on the contrary, produces greater problems, and sometimes tragic consequences. Denying a disease does not cure it; it makes it worse.

Let's try now to problematize some social phenomenon. Undoubtedly, we will not plumb the full depths of its complexity, but we can get an idea of the degree of simplification with which it is treated on a daily basis, and not always innocently.

Let's start with a brief example. Consider the case of a man who rapes and kills a young girl. I take this example not only because it is, along with torture, one of the most abhorrent crimes imaginable, but because it represents a common criminal practice in all societies, even those that boast of their special moral virtues.

First of all, we have a crime. Beyond the semantics of "crime" and "punishment," we can evaluate the act on its own merits, without, that is, needing to recur to a genealogy of the criminal and of his victim, or needing to research the origins of the criminal's conduct. Both the rape and the murder should be punished by the law, and by the rest of society. And period. On this view, there is no room for discussion.

Very well. Now let's imagine that in a given country the number of rapes and murders doubles in a particular year and then doubles again the year after that. A simplification would be to reduce the new phenomenon to the criminal deed described above. That is to say, a simplification would be to understand that the solution to the problem would be to not let a single one of these crimes go unpunished. Stated in a third way, a simplification would be to not recognize the social realities behind the individual criminal act. A more in-depth analysis of the first case could reveal to us a painful childhood, marked by the sexual abuse of the future abuser, of the future criminal. This observation would not in any way overturn the criminality of the deed itself, just as evaluated above, but it would allow us to begin to see the complexity of a problem that a simplification threatens to perpetuate. Starting from this psychological analysis of the individual, we could certainly continue on to observe other kinds of implications arising from the same criminal's circumstances, such as, for example, the economic conditions of a specific social underclass, its exploitation and moral stigmatization by the rest of society, the moral violence and humiliation of its misery, its scales of moral value constructed in accordance with an apparatus of production, reproduction and contradictory consumption, by social institutions like a public education system that helps the poor less than it humiliates them, certain religious organizations that have created sin for the poor while using the latter to earn Paradise for themselves, the mass media, advertising, labor contradictions… and so on.

We can understand terrorism in our time in the same way. The criminality of an act of terrorism is not open to discussion (or it shouldn't be). Killing is always a disgrace, a historical curse. But killing innocents and on a grand scale can have no justification or pardon of any kind. Therefore, to renounce punishment for those who promote terrorism is an act of cowardice and a flagrant concession to impunity.

Nevertheless, we should also remember here our initial caveat. Understanding a social and historical phenomenon as a consequence of the existence of "bad guys" on Earth is an extremely naive simplification or, to the contrary, an ideologically astute simplification that, by avoiding integrated analysis—historical, economic, political—exempts the administrators of the meaning of "bad": the good guys.

We will not even begin to analyze, in these brief reflections, how one comes to identify one particular group and not others with the qualifier "terrorist." For that let it suffice to recommend a reading of Roland Barthes—to mention just one classic source. We will assume the restricted meaning of the term, which is the one assumed by the press and the mainstream political narratives.

Even so, if we resort to the idea that terrorism exists because criminals exist in the world, we would have to think that in recent times there has been an especially abundant harvest of wicked people. (An idea explicitly present in the official discourse of all the governments of countries affected by the phenomenon.) But if it were true that in our world today there are more bad people than before, surely it isn't by the grace of God but via historical developments that such a phenomenon has come to be. No historical circumstance is produced by chance, and therefore, to believe that killing terrorists will eliminate terrorism from the world is not only a foolish simplification but, by denying a historical origin for the problem, by presenting it as ahistorical, as purely a product of Evil, even as a struggle between two theological "essences" removed from any social, economic and political context, provokes a tragic worsening of the situation. It is a way of not confronting the problem, of not attacking its deep roots.

On many occasions violence is unavoidable. For example, if someone attacks us it would seem legitimate to defend ourselves with an equal degree of violence. Certainly a true Christian would offer the other cheek before instigating a violent reaction; however, if he were to respond violently to an act of aggression no one could deny him the right, even though he might be contradicting one of the commandments of Christ. But if a person or a government tells us that violence will be diminished by unleashing violence against the bad guys—affecting the innocent in the process—not only does this deny the search for a cause for the violence, it also will serve to strengthen it, or at least legitimate it, in the eyes of those who suffer the consequences.

Punishing those responsible for the violence is an act of justice. Claiming that violence exists only because violent people exist is an act of ignorance or of ideological manipulation.

If one continues to simplify the problem, insisting that it consists of a conflict produced by the "incompatibility" of two religious views—as if one of them had not been present for centuries—as if it were a matter of a simple kind of war where victory is achieved only with the total defeat of the enemy, one will drag the entire world into an intercontinental war. If one genuinely seeks the social origin and motivation of the problem—the "why"—and acts to eliminate and attenuate it, we will most assuredly witness a relaxing of the tension that is currently escalating. We will not see the end of violence and injustice in the world, but at least misfortune of unimaginable proportions will be avoided.

The analysis of the "origin of violence" would be useless if it were produced and consumed only within a university. It should be a problem for the headlines, a problem to be discussed dispassionately in the bars and in the streets. At the same time, we will have to recognize, once again, that we need a genuine dialogue. Not a return to the diplomatic farce, but a dialogue between peoples who have begun dangerously to see one another as enemies, as threats—a disagreement, really, based on a profound and crushing ignorance of the other and of oneself. What is urgent is a painful but courageous dialogue, where each one of us might recognize our prejudice and our self-centeredness. A dialogue that dispenses with the religious fanaticism—both Muslim and Christian—so in vogue these days, with its messianic and moralizing pretensions. A dialogue, in short, to spite the deaf who refuse to hear.

According to the true believers and the true religion, there can be only one true God, God. Some claim that the true God is One and he is Three at the same time, but judging by the evidence, God is One and Many more. The true God is unique but with different politics according to the interests of the true believers. Each one is the true God, each one moves the faithful against the faithful of other gods, which are always false gods even though each one is someone's true God. Each true God organizes the virtue of each virtuous people on the basis of true customs and the true Morality. There is only one Morality based on the true God, but since there is more than one true God there is also more than one true Morality, only one of which is truly true.

But, how do we know which one is the true truth? The proper methods for proof are disputable; what is not disputed is the current practice: scorn, threats, oppression and, when in doubt, death. True death is always the final and inevitable recourse of the true truth, which comes from the true God, in order to save the true Morality and, above all, the true believers.

Yes, at times I have my doubts about what is true, and I know that doubt has been condemned by all religions, by all theologies, and by all political discourses. At times I have my doubts, but it is likely that God does not hold my doubt in contempt. He must be very busy concerning himself with so much certainty, so much pride, so much morality, behind so many ministers who have taken control of his word, holding Him hostage in a building somewhere so as to be able to conduct their business in public without obstacles.

(2003)

The Jesus the Emperors Kidnapped

Who will lend me a ladder
to climb up the timbering,
to remove all the nails from
Jesus the Nazarene?
(Antonio Machado)

In 2007, the president of Venezuela, Hugo Chávez, referred to Jesus as the greatest socialist in history. I was not interested in making a defense or an attack on his person. At that time, I only made a few observations about a typical reaction caused by his words throughout different parts of the world.

Perhaps saying that Jesus was a socialist is like saying that Tutankhamen was Egyptian or Seneca was Spanish. It remains a semantic imprecision. Nevertheless, regarding those who recently approached me with a look of horror on their faces as a result of the words of the "bad boy," did they do so on the basis of some reasoning or simply on the basis of the codes imposed by a dominant discourse?

Personally, I have always been uncomfortable with power accumulated in just one man. But although Mr. Chávez is a powerful man in his country, he is not the one responsible for the current state of the world. For an elite few, the best state possible. For most, the source of physical and, above all, moral violence.

If it is a scandal to imagine Jesus to be socialist, why is it not, then, to associate him and compromise him with capitalist culture and ethics? If it is a scandal to associate Jesus with the eternal rebel, why is it not, in contrast, to associate him with the interests of successive empires—with the exception of the ancient Roman Empire? Those who do not argue the sacredness of capitalism are, in large number, fervent followers of Jesus. Better said, of a particular and convenient image of Jesus. In certain cases not only followers of his word, but administrators of his message.

All of us, or almost all of us, are in favor of certain economic development. Nonetheless, why is social justice always confused with economic development? Why is that Christian theology that considers economic success, wealth, to be the divine sign of having been chosen to enter Paradise, even if through the eye of a needle, so widely disseminated?

Conservatives are right: it is a simplification to reduce Jesus to his political dimension. But their reasoning becomes manipulation when it denies categorically any political value in his action, at the same time that his image is used and his values are invoked to justify a determined politics. It is political to deny politics in any church. It is political to presume political neutrality.

An observer who passively witnesses the torture or rape of another person is not neutral. Even less neutral is he who does not even want to watch and turns his head to pray. Because if he who remains silent concedes, he who is indifferent legitimates.

The confirmation of a *status quo* that benefits one social class and keeps others submerged is political. The sermon that favors the power of men and keeps women under their will and convenience is political. The mere mention of Jesus or Mohammed before, during and after justifying a war, a killing, a dictatorship, the extermination of a people or of a lone individual is terribly political.

Lamentably, although politics is not everything, everything is political. Therefore, one of the most hypocritical forms of politics is to assert that some social action exists in this world that might be apolitical. We might attribute to animals this marvelous innocence, if we did not know that even communities of monkeys and of other mammals are governed not only by a clear negotiation of powers but, even, by a history that establishes ranks and privileges. Which ought to be sufficient to diminish somewhat the pride of those oppressors who consider themselves different from orangutans because of the sophisticated technology of their power.

Many years ago I wrote about the political factor in the death of Jesus. That his death was contaminated by politics does not take away from his religious value but quite the contrary. If the son of God descended to the imperfect world of men and immersed himself in a concrete society, an oppressed society, acquiring all of the human limitations, why would he have to do so ignoring one of the principle factors of that society which was, precisely, a political factor of resistance?

Why was Jesus born in a poor home and one of scarce religious orientation? Why was he not born in the home of a rich and educated Pharisee? Why did he live almost his entire life in a small, peripheral town, as was Nazareth, and not in the capital of the Roman Empire or in the religious capital, Jerusalem? Why did he go to Jerusalem, the center of political power at the time, to bother, to challenge power in the name of the most universal human salvation and dignity? As a xenophobe from today would say: if he didn't like the order of things in the center of the world, he shouldn't have gone there to cause trouble.

We must remember that it was not the Jews who killed Jesus but the Romans. Those Romans who have nothing to do with the present day inhabitants of Italy, other than the name. Someone might argue that the Jews condemned him for religious reasons. I am not saying that religious reasons did not exist, but that these do not exclude other, political, reasons: the Jewish upper class, like almost all the upper classes of peoples dominated by foreign empires, found itself in a relationship of privilege that led it to a complacent diplomacy with the Roman Empire. This is what happened also in America, in the times of the Conquest. The Romans, in contrast, had no religious reason for taking care of the problem of that rebel from Nazareth. Their reasons were eminently political: Jesus represented a grave threat to the peaceful order established by the empire.

Now, if we are going to discuss Jesus' political options, we might refer to the texts canonized after the first Council of Nicea, nearly three hundred years after his death. The theological and political result of this founding Council may be questionable. That is to say, if the life of Jesus developed in the conflict against the political power of his time, if the writers of the Gospels, somewhat later, suffered similar persecutions, we cannot say the same about those religious men who gathered in the year 325 by order of an emperor, Constantine, who sought to stabilize and unify his empire, without leaving aside for this purpose other means, like the assassination of his political adversaries.

Let us suppose that all of this is not important. Besides, there are very debatable points. Let us take the facts of the religious documents that remain to us from that historical moment. What do we see there?

The son of God being born in an animal stable. The son of God working in the modest carpentry trade of his father. The son of God surrounded by poor people, by women of ill repute, by sick people, by marginalized beings of every type. The son of God expelling the merchants from the temple. The son of God asserting that it would be easier for a camel to pass through the eye of a needle than for a rich man to ascend to the kingdom of heaven (probably the Greek word *kamel* did not mean *camel* but an enormous rope that was used in the ports to tie up the boats, but the translation error has not altered the idea of the metaphor). The son of God questioning, denying the alleged nationalism of God. The son of God rising above the old and cruel laws, like the penalty of death by stoning of an adulterous woman. The son of God separating the things of Ceasar from the things of the Father. The son of God valuing the coin of a widow above the traditional donations of the rich and famous. The son of God condemning religious pride, the economic and moral ostentation of men. The son of God entering into Jerusalem on a humble donkey. The son of God confronting religious and political power, the Pharisees of the Law and the imperial hells of the moment. The son of God defamed and humiliated, dying under military torture, surrounded by a few followers, mostly women. The son of God taking an unquestionable stand for the poor, for the weak and the marginalized by power, for the universalization of the human condition, on earth as much as in heaven.

An unlikely profile for a capitalist who dedicates six days of the week to the accumulation of money and half a day to clean his conscience in church; who exercises a strange *compassion* (so different from *solidarity*) that consists in helping the world by imposing his own views like it or not.

Even though Jesus may be today the principal instrument of conservatives who grasp at power, it is still difficult to maintain that he was not a revolutionary. To be precise he did not die as a result of having been complacent with the political power of the moment. Power does not kill or torture its bootlickers; it rewards them. For the others remains the greater prize: dignity. And I believe that few if any figures in history show more dignity and commitment with all of humanity than Jesus of Nazareth, who one day will have to be brought down from the cross.

(2007)

Do You Believe in God? Yes or No

Someone asks me whether I believe in God and indicates that a one sentence answer will do. Two at the most. It's easy, yes or no.

I'm sorry, but why do you insist on subjecting me to the tyranny of such a question? If you are truly interested in my response, you will have to hear me out. If not, good day to you. No hard feelings.

The question, like so many others, is tricky. It demands of me a clear *yes* or a clear *no*. I would have one of those very clear answers if the god about whom I am being asked were so clear and well defined. Do you like Santiago? Excuse me, which Santiago? Santiago de Compostela in Spain or Santiago, Chile? Santiago del Estero in Argentina or Santiago Matamoros?

Okay, look, my greatest desire is for God to exist. It's the only thing I ask of him. But not just any god. It seems like almost everyone agrees that there is only one God, but if that is true then one must recognize that this is a god with multiple personalities, from multiple religions and with mutual hatred for one another.

The truth is that I cannot believe in a god who inflames the heart for war and who inspires such fear that nobody is capable of making even the slightest change. Which is why dying and killing for that lie is common practice; questioning it a rare heresy. I cannot believe, and much less support, a god who orders people massacred, who is made to the measure and convenience of some nations above others, of some social classes above others, of some genders above others, of some races above others. A god who for his own entertainment has created some men to be condemned from birth and others to be the select few until death, and a god who, at the same time, is praised for his universality and infinite love.

How does one believe in such a selfish, such a mean-spirited god? A criminal god who condemns greed and the accumulation of money and rewards the chosen greedy ones with greater material wealth. How does one believe in a god of neckties on Sunday, who shouts and swells with blood condemning those who don't believe in such an apparatus of war and domination? How does one believe in a god who instead of liberating subjugates, punishes, and condemns? How does one believe in a small-minded god who needs the petty politics of a few of the faithful in order to gain votes? How does one believe in a mediocre god who must use bureaucracy on Earth to administer his business in Heaven? How does one believe in a god who allows himself to be manipulated like a child frightened in the night and who every day serves the most repugnant interests on Earth? How does one believe in a god who draws mysterious images on dank walls in order to announce to humanity that we are living in a time of hatreds and wars? How does one believe in a god who communicates through street-corner charlatans who promise Heaven and threaten Hell to passersby, as if they were real estate agents?

Which god are we talking about when we talk about the One and All-Powerful God? Is this the same God who sends fanatics to immolate themselves in a market, the same God who sends planes to discharge Hell on children and innocents in his name? Perhaps so. Then, I don't believe in that god. Rather, I don't want to believe that such a criminal could be a supernatural force. Because we already have our hands full with our own human wickedness. It's just that human evil would not be so hypocritical if it were to focus on oppressing and killing in its own name and not in the name of a kind and creative god.

A God who allows his manipulators—who have no peace in their hearts—to speak of the infinite peace of God while they go around condemning those without faith. Condemning those who have no faith in that tragic madness attributed every day to God. Men and women without peace who claim to be chosen by God and who go around proclaiming this because it's not enough for them that God would have chosen them for their doubtful virtues. Those terrorists of the soul who go about threatening with Hell—sometimes softly and sometimes shouting—anybody who dares to doubt so much madness.

A God, creator of the Universe, who must fit between the narrow walls of consecrated homes and buildings uncursed by man, not so that God has a place but so that God can be put in a place. In a proper place, which is to say, privatized, controlled, circumscribed to a few ideas, a few paragraphs, and at the service of a sect of the self-selected.

Of course, the classic accusation, established by tradition, for all those who would doubt the real attributes of God is arrogance. The furious preachers, in contrast, do not stop for an instant to reflect upon the infinite arrogance of their claim to belong to, and even guide and administer, the select club of those chosen by the Creator.

The only thing I ask of God is that he exist. But every time I see these celestial hordes I am reminded of the story, true or fictitious, of the indigenous chieftain Hatuey, condemned to be burned alive by the governor of Cuba, Diego Velásquez. According to father Bartolomé de las Casas, a priest was present for Hatuey's final hours, offering him Heaven if he converted to Christianity. The chieftain asked if white men could be found there. "Yes," responded the priest, "because they believe in God." Which was sufficient reason for the rebel chief to refuse to accept the new truth.

So, if God is that being who walks behind his followers in a trance, in all truthfulness, I cannot believe in him. Why would the Creator confer critical reason on his creatures and then demand of them blind obedience, hallucinatory trembling, uncontrollable hatreds? Why would God prefer believers over thinkers? Why must seeing the light mean losing consciousness? Could it be that innocence and obedience get along well?

(2006)

The Imperfect Sex. Why Is Sor Juana Not a Saint?

Every hegemonic power in every historical period establishes the limits of what is normal and, consequently, of what is natural. Thus, the power that organized patriarchal society also reserved for itself (and still reserves for itself) the unquestionable right to define what was a man and what was a woman. Every time some exalted person takes recourse to the mediocre argument that "things have been like this since the beginning of the world," he situates the origin of the world in a recent period of the history of humanity.

Like any system, patriarchy fulfilled an organizing function. Probably, at some moment, it was an order convenient to the majority of society, including women. I don't believe that oppression arises from patriarchy, but instead when the latter attempts to perpetuate itself by imposing itself on processes that range from the survival to the liberation of human kind. If patriarchy was once a logical system of values for an agricultural system of production and survival, today it no longer means anything more than an oppressive, and for some time now, hypocritical tradition.

In 1583, the revered Fray Luis de León wrote *La perfecta casada* (*The Perfect Wife*) as a book of useful advice for marriage. There, as with any other text of the tradition, it is understood that an exceptionally virtuous woman is a manly woman. "What here we call woman of principle; and we might say manly woman (…) means virtue of spirit and strength of heart, industry and wealth and power." Then: "in the man to be gifted with understanding and reason, does not make him worthy of praise, because having this is *his own nature* (…) If the truth be told, it is a bouquet of dishonesties for the chaste woman to think she could not be so, or that in being so she does something for which she should be thanked." Then: "God, when he decided to marry man by giving him woman, said: 'Let us make for him a help mate' (Gen. 2); from whence it is understood that *the natural place of woman and the end for which God created her, is for her to be a helper to her husband.*" A hundred years before Sor Juana would be condemned for speaking too much and for defending her right to speak, the nature of woman was *well defined*: "it is right for [women] to pride themselves on being silent, both those for whom it is convenient to cover up their lack of knowledge, and those who might shamelessly reveal what they know, because in all of them it is not only an agreeable condition, but *a proper virtue, to speak little and be silent.*" Then: "because, just as *nature*, as we have said and will say, made women to remain in the home as its keepers, so also it obliged them to keep their mouths closed. (…) Just as the good and honest woman was not made by nature for the study of the sciences nor for negotiation of hardships, but for a simple and domestic profession, *it also limited their understanding*, and therefore it rationed their words and reason." But the moralizer of the day was not lacking in tenderness: "do not think that God created them and gave them to man only for them to keep the home, but also *to console him and give him joy. So that in her the tired and angry husband might find rest, and the children love, and the family piety, and all of them generally an agreeable refuge*."

By the next century, Francisco Cascales believed that woman had to struggle against her nature, which was not only determined but evil or defective besides: "The needle and the distaff"—wrote the military man and university professor, in 1653—"are the woman's weapons, and so strong, that armed with them she will resist the most prideful enemy to tempt her." Which amounted to saying that the distaff was the weapon of an oppressive system.

Juan de Zabaleta, notable figure of the Spanish Golden Age, declared in 1653 that "in poetry there is no substance; nor in the understanding of a woman." And later: "woman is *naturally* gossipy," the woman poet "adds more madness to her madness (…) The woman poet is the most imperfect and abhorrent animal formed by nature (…) If it were permitted of me, I would burn her alive. He who celebrates a woman for being a poet, God should give her to him as a wife, so that he might know what he celebrates." In his following book, the lawyer wrote: "the word wife means comfort more than anything, pleasure the least."

Nonetheless, man "by adoring a woman takes adoration away from the Creator." Zabaleta at times goes so far as to create metaphors with a certain aesthetic value: the woman in church "with her fan in hand enlivens with its air the fire that encircles her." (1654)

In 1575, the physician Juan Huarte informed us that the testicles affirm the temperament more than the heart, while in the woman "the organ that is most gripped by the alterations of the uterus, according to all the physicians, is the brain, although there may be no grounds on which to base this correspondence." Hippocrates, Galeno, Sigmund Freud and the most fanatical supporters of the Boca Juniors soccer team would all agree. The wise and ingenious man, according to the Spanish physician, has a son with contrary traits when the woman's seed predominates, and *no wise child can come from a woman.* For this reason, when the man predominates, even when he is brutish and stupid a clever son results.

In his book about Fernando (a.k.a. the Catholic Monarch Ferdinand), another renowned moralist, Baltasar Gracián, dedicates some final lines to Queen Isabella. "What most aided Fernando"—wrote the Jesuit—"[was] doña Isabella his Catholic consort, that great princess who*, even though a woman, exceeded the limits of a man.*" Although there were noteworthy women, "commonly in this sex the passions reign in such a way that they leave no room for counsel, for patience, for prudence, essential parts of government, and with power their tyranny is augmented.

(…) Ordinarily, manly women were very prudent." Later: "In Spain manly females have always endured a position for males, and in the house of Austria they have always been respected and employed." (1641)

I believe that the idea of the manly woman as virtuous woman is consistent with the tolerance of lesbianism by the same patriarchal system of values that condemned masculine homosexuality to burn at the stake, whether in the Middle East, in Europe or among the imperial Incas. Where there was a greater predominance for matriarchy, neither the virginity of the woman nor the homosexuality of men was watched over with such fervor.

A famous woman—beatified, sainted and given a doctorate by the Catholic Church—Saint Teresa, wrote in 1578: "Weakness is natural and it is very weak, especially in women." Recommending an extreme discipline with the nuns, the future saint argued: "I do not believe there is anything in the world that could damage a prelate more than to not be feared, and for his subjects to think they may deal with him as with an equal, especially for women, for once understanding that there is in the prelate such softness... *governing them will be difficult.*" But this deficient nature impeded not only the proper social order but mystical achievement as well. Just like Buddha, in her famous book *Las moradas* the same saint recognized the natural "stupidity of women" that made it difficult for them to reach the center of the divine mystery.

It is perfectly understandable that a woman at the service of the patriarchal order, like Saint Teresa, would have been beatified, while another religious woman who openly opposed this structure would never have been recognized as such. I would sum up Saint Teresa's slogan in just one word: obedience, above all social obedience.

Saint Teresa died an old woman and without the martyrdom proper to the saints. Sor Juana, in contrast, was made to suffer psychological, moral and, finally, physical torture until she died at the age of fourty-four, serving her fellow man in the epidemic of 1695. But none of that matters for canonizing her as a saint when "the worst of all women" committed the sin of questioning authority. Why not propose, then, *Saint Juana Inés de la Cruz*, patron saint of oppressed women?

Those who reject Sor Juana's religious merits adduce a political value in her figure, when not merely a literary one. In another essay we already noted the political value of the life and death of Jesus, a value historically denied. The political and the aesthetic in Santa Teresa—the "patron saint of writers"—fill her works and thoughts as much as the religious and the mystical do. Nonetheless, a hegemonic political position is an invisible politics: it is omnipresent. Only that politics which resists the hegemony, which contests the dominant discourse becomes visible.

When I kiss my wife on the mouth in a public square, I am exercising a hegemonic sexuality, which is the heterosexual one. If two women or two men do the same thing they are not only exercising their homosexuality but also a challenge to a hegemonic order that rewards some and punishes others. Each time a man goes out on the street dressed as a traditional woman, inevitably he is making a—visible—political statement. I also make a political statement when I go out on the street dressed as a (traditional) man, but my declaration coincides with the hegemonic politics, is transparent, invisible, appears apolitical, neutral. It is for this reason that the act of the marginalized becomes a visible politics.

We can understand in the same way the political and religious factor in two women as different as Saint Teresa and Sor Juana. Perhaps this is one of the reasons for which one of them has been repeatedly honored by the religious tradition and the other reduced to the literary circle or to the Mexican two hundred-peso notes, a symbol of the material world, an abstraction of sin.

(2006)

V. Latin America

Why the name "Latin America"?

The essentialist component of the ancestral search for identity by nationalist projects—which has kept intellectuals busy for so long, Octavio Paz being one of them—has not completely disappeared or has turned into a commercial relationship between competing signs in a new global context. And as usual, reality is a byproduct of ambiguities in its own representations.

What does "Latin" mean? For many years, the typical Latin American—which is another way to say "the stereotypical Latin American"—has been represented by the indigenous person of Aztec, Maya, Inca, or Quechua origin, who preserves their ancestral traditions and mixes them with the Catholic rites. The Castilian language and the violence of colonization was what these peoples had in common. However, to European and North American eyes, and even to their own eyes, they were monolithically defined as "Latin Americans". Those who lived in the region of Río de la Plata were called by Anglo Saxons "Southern Europeans".

If we go back to the etymology of the word "Latin," we will find a striking contradiction in this aforementioned identification:

none of the indigenous cultures encountered by the Spaniards in the new continent had any connection to "Latin." By contrast, regions to the south lacked this indigenous ethnic and cultural component. Overwhelmingly, the population and culture of the south came from Italy, France, Spain, and Portugal.

In *Valiente Mundo Nuevo* (*Brave New World*), Carlos Fuentes tells us: "We are in the first place a multiracial, policultural continent. For this reason, the term 'Latin American,' invented by the French in the 19th century to include themselves in the American territory, is not employed. The most complete description is used instead: Indo-Afro-Iberian-America. But in any case, the Indian and the African components are present, implicit."

To this objection of the Mexican essayist, Koen de Munter responds in kind, observing that indigenist discourse has become fashionable as long as it refers to the defense of certain politically harmless, folkloric groups, so as to forget the great masses of people who migrate to the cities and camouflage themselves in a kind of compulsory *mestizaje*. This *mestizaje* (or racial mixing), in countries like Mexico, would be the central metaphor of a national project that began in the 90s. Fuentes believes that we were lucky to be colonized by the Spanish and not by the English, which gave rise to this racial mixing on the continent. But Koen de Munter understands this discourse to be part of a "hispanophile" demagogy, a "mixed race ideology" as a result of which the unacceptable conditions of current Latin American reality are overlooked. According to the author himself, hispanophilia makes these intellectuals forget about the colonial racism of the Spain that fought the Moors and the Jews as they made their way into the new continent. In short, rather than mestizaje or racial mixing, we should talk about "multiple violation".

Maybe because the proposed term was too long, Carlos Fuentes decided to use "Ibero-America", this one being, in my view, more restrictive than the one "interestedly" suggested by the French, since it excludes not only the waves of French migration to the southern hemisphere and to other regions of the continent in question; it also excludes other even more numerous immigrants, who were as Latin as the Iberian peoples: the Italians. It should suffice to remember that, by the end of the 19th century, eighty percent of the Buenos Aires population was Italian, as a result of which someone defined the Argentineans—again generalizing—as "Spanish speaking Italians".

On the other hand, the idea of including the indigenous component ("Indo") together with the name "America" implies that they are two different things. A similar problem is encountered with the modest and "politically correct" racial reference "African-American" to refer to a dark- skinned North American who is about as African as Clint Eastwood or Kim Basinger. We might think that indigenous peoples have the greatest right to reclaim the name of "Americans", but the term has been colonized just like the land, the physical and cultural space. Even today, when we say "American" we refer to the people from a specific country: The United States of America. As for the meaning of this term, it is equally important to define what it means as it is to define what it does not mean. And this definition of its semantic borders is derived not only from its etymology, but from a semantic dispute in which the exclusion of all that is not of the U.S. has won out. A Cuban or a Brazilian could provide a long list of reasons why they too should be called "Americans", but the redefinition of this term is not established based on the intellectual will of some, but by force of cultural and cross-cultural tradition. Although the first creoles who lived south of the Rio Grande, from Mexico to the Rio de la Plata, called themselves "Americans", the geopolitical power of the United States grabbed this term, forcing the rest to use an adjective in order to differentiate themselves.

This simplification may also be the result of the predominance of the perspective of the other: of the European. Europe, like the United States, has been historically selfish and egomaniacal, as have been the colonized peoples. Few in America, without an important ideological purpose, have esteemed and studied indigenous cultures as much as they have European culture. That is, our simplified and simplifying definitions of "Latin America" may be the result of the natural confusion that the other´s gaze projects: all Indians are the same: Mayans, Aztecs, Incans, and Guaranies. In Mexico alone there was—and is—a cultural mosaic that only our ignorance can confuse and group together under the term "indigenous". These differences were frequently resolved by going to war or by sacrificing the other.

Anyway, even if Latin America is considered an extension of the West (as the far West), its names and identities have mainly represented a negation, since the 19th century. In July 1946 Jorge Luis Borges observed, in the journal *Sur* (South), this same cultural habit with regard to Argentineans. Nationalists, "ignore, however, the Argentineans; in polemics they prefer to define them in relation to some external fact; as the Spanish conquerors (let us say) or some imaginary Catholic or Anglo-Saxon imperialist tradition."

Latin American republics were successive literary inventions of the intellectual élite of the 19th century. Defining, prescribing, and naming are not minor details. But reality also exists, and it never completely adapted to their definitions, despite the violence of the imagination. The difference between the concept and the reality of the people sometimes was as large as centuries-old injustices, exclusions, and violent revolts and rebellions, which never achieved the status of revolutions. What is represented remains weaker than its Representation.

(2004)

Violence of the Master, Violence of the Slave

For some reason, the phrase "violence begets violence" was popularized the world over at the same time that its implicit meaning was kept restricted to the violence of the oppressed. That is to say, the master's violence over the slave is invisible in a state of slavery, just as in a state of oppression the force that sustains it uses every (ideological) means in order not to lose this status of invisibility or—in case of exposure— of naturalness.

Within that invisible or natural frame, the Cuban slave Juan Manzano referred nostalgically to his first masters: "I had there the same Madam Joaquina who treated me like a child, she would dress me, groom me and take care that I not come in contact with the other little black boys at the same table like when with the Marquess Lady Justis I was given my plate at the feet of my Lady the Marquess." Then came the bad times, when the young Juan was punished by imprisonment, hunger and torture. Once the punishment was finished, he ate "without measure" and for this sin he was punished again. "Not a few times have I suffered by the hand of a black man vigorous whippings," he recalled in his *Autobiography of a Slave* (1839), which demonstrates the perfection of oppression even in a primitive state of production and education.

This type of slavery was abolished in the written laws of almost all of Latin America in the early 19th century. But slavery of the same kind was continued in practice until the 20th century. The Ecuadorian Juan Montalvo warned "the Indians are free by law, but how can one deny it? They are slaves by abuse and custom." And then: "they give him the stick so he will remember and return for another beating. And the Indian returns, because that is his condition, that when he is whipped, trembling on the ground, he gets up thanking his tormenter: *'Diu su lu pagui, amu.'* [*God bless you, Master*] Races oppressed and reviled for three hundred years need eight hundred more to return to themselves."

For his part, the Bolivian Alcides Arguedas, in *Pueblo enfermo* (*A Sick People*, 1909), recognized that the landed elite of his country refused to develop the freight train because the Indians carried their harvests from one region to another for free and, as if that were not enough, the honesty of the Indians made them incapable of stealing someone else's oxen. This example alone would be enough to demonstrate that the ideologies of the dominant classes insinuate themselves into the morality of the oppressed (the way the fact that an illiterate might handle complex grammatical rules demonstrates the existence of an unconscious knowledge). Another Arguedas, the Peruvian José María Arguedas, left us a living portrait of this culture of the Indian-servant, the unsalaried freed slave, in *Los ríos profundos* (Deep Rivers, 1958).

According to the Bolivian Alcides Arguedas, the soldiers would take the Indians by the hair and drag them off under threat of the saber to clean their barracks, or steal their sheep in order to maintain the army troops as they passed through. So that it be clear to us that oppression makes use of all possible institutions, in the same book we read a citation from the period which informed, with reference to one of those condemned by history, that "*the ox and his seven year old son are impounded* by the priest due to the costs of the burial of his wife." And further along: "Exasperated, dispirited, physically and morally spent, incapable of attempting the violent assertion of its rights, the indigenous race has given itself over to alcoholism in alarming fashion. […] The Indian is never seen laughing except when he is inebriated. […] His soul is a repository of rancor accumulated from long ago, since the moment when, the flower of the race sealed up, against its will, in the depth of the mines, he rapidly withered, without provoking mercy in anyone. […] Today, ignorant, degraded, miserable, he is the object of general exploitation and general antipathy." Until one day he explodes "listening to his soul replete with hatreds, vents his passions and robs, kills, murders with atrocious brutality." And since violence cannot occur with impunity, "the soldiers go out well munitioned; they shoot down as many as they can; they rob, rape, spread fear and terror wherever they go." In this culture of oppression, the woman can be no better: "rough and awkward, she feels loved when beaten by the male; otherwise, for her a man has no value."

A year later, in various articles appearing in daily newspapers of La Paz and collected in the book *Creación de la pedagogía nacional* (Creation of National Pedagogy), Franz Tamayo responds to some of Arguedas' conclusions and confirms others: "work, justice, glory, it is all lies, it is all lies in Bolivia; everyone lies, except the one who does not speak, the one who works and is silent: the Indian." Then: "Even whites of a certain status spoke of a divine curse, and the priests of the small towns and villages spread rumors among their ignorant Indian parishioners of God's anger at the fallen race and his desire to make it disappear due to its lack of obedience, submissiveness and obsequiousness." (1910) Needless to say, instead of *Bolivia* we could write the name of any other Latin American country and we would not do violence to the truth of the statement.

The master is visualized as a pure and generous being when he concedes an unusual benefit to the slave, as if he possessed a divine power to administer the rights of another. Perhaps we might accept a certain *kindness of the oppressor* if we were to consider a particular context. The point is that we do not demand of the old feudal subjects that they think like us; we demand from ourselves that we not think like the old feudal subjects, as if there existed no historical experience in between.

From a humanistic point of view, the violence of the slave is always engendered by the violence of the master and not the other way around. But when we impose the idea that the violence of the slave engenders more violence, we are equating what is not equal in order to maintain an order that, in fact and in its discourse, denies the very notion of human equality.

For this reason, just as during the mid-twentieth century reactionaries of all kinds associated, strategically, racial integration with communism in order to justify apartheid as a social system, today also they associate humanist principles with a specific left politics. Conservatives cannot comprehend that part of their so frequently mentioned *personal responsibility* is to think globally and collectively. Otherwise, personal responsibility is just selfishness, which is to say, moral irresponsibility.

If as recently as 1972 Rene Dubos coined the famous phrase, “Think globally, act locally,” reactionary thought has always practiced an inverse moral formula: “Think locally, act globally.” In other words, think provincially about the interests of your own village, your own class, and act like an imperialist who is going to save civilization as if he were the armed hand of God.

If the masters insist so much on the benefits of competition, why do they demand so much cooperation from the slaves? Because one needs something more than all the weapons in the world in order to force an entire people into submission: it is the *demoralization of the oppressed*, the ideology of the master, the fear of the slave and the collaboration of the rest of the people that function as the fulcrum for the lever of oppression. Otherwise, one could not comprehend how a few thousand Spanish adventurers conquered and dominated millions of Incans and Aztecs and destroyed centuries-old sophisticated cultures.

In many moments of history, from the so-called independence of the American countries to the liberation of the slaves, frequently the only solution was the use of violence. It remains to be determined whether this resource is always effective or, on occasion, only aggravates the initial problem.

I suspect that there exists historically a *coefficient of critical progression* that depends on the material possibilities of the moment—technical and economic—and on the mental, moral and cultural maturity of a people. An ideal state for humanism, in accordance with its development since the 15th century, should be a perfect anarchist social state. Nevertheless, to pretend to eliminate the force and violence of the State without having achieved the requisite technical and moral development would not make us advance toward that utopia but rather the opposite; we would be set back several centuries. Both a revolutionary advance that aims to by-pass that parameter of *critical progression* and a conservative reaction lead us to the historical frustration of humanity as a whole. I am afraid that there are recent examples in Latin America where the oppressor even organized the violence of the oppressed in order to legitimate and conserve the oppressor's privileges. This refinement of the techniques of domination has a purpose. At a point in history when the population matters, not only in systems of representative democracy but, even, in some dictatorships, the construction of *public opinion* is a key chess piece, the most important, in the strategy of the dominant elites. Not by accident was the poorly-named universalization of the vote in the 19th century a way of maintaining the status quo: with scarce instruction, the population was easy to manipulate, especially easy when it believed that the *caudillos* were elected by them and not by a previously constructed discourse of the oligarchy, a discourse that included ideolexicons like, *fatherland*, *honor*, *order*, and *freedom*.

(2006)

ONE BOLIVIA, WHITE AND WEALTHY

The rapid Conquest of Amerindia would have been impossible without the Mesoamerican and Andean cosmology. Otherwise two mature empires, with millions of inhabitants and brave armies would never have succumbed to the madness of a handful of Spaniards. But it was also possible due to the new adventurer and warrior spirit of the medieval culture of a Spanish Crown victorious in the Reconquest of Spain, and the new capitalist spirit of the Renaissance. From a strictly military point of view, neither Cortés nor Pizarro would be remembered today if it had not been for the bad faith of two empires like the Aztec of Moctezuma and the Incan of Atahualpa. Both knew they were illegitimate, and this weighed upon them in a manner that it weighs upon no modern governor.

The Spaniards first conquered these imperial heads or crushed them and cut them off in order to replace them with puppet chiefs, privileging the old native aristocracy, a story that may seem very familiar to any peripheral nation of the 21st century.

The principal strategic legacy of this history was progressive social and geographic division. While at first the cultural revolution of the United States, based on utopian theories, was admired and then later simply its muscular power, which resulted from unions and annexations, the America of the south proceeded with the inverse method of divisions. Thus, were destroyed the dreams of those men who today are called liberators, like Simón Bolívar, José Artigas or San Martín. Thus, Central America and South America exploded into the fragments of tiny nations. This fragmentation was convenient for the nascent empires of the Industrial Revolution and of the celebrated Creole *caudillismo*, whereby a chief representative of the feudal agrarian culture would impose himself above the law and humanist progress in order to rescue the prosperity of his class, which he confused with the prosperity of the new country. Paradoxically, as in the imperial democracy of the Athens of Pericles, both the British and American empires were administered differently, as representative democracies. Paradoxically, while the discourse of the wealthy classes in Latin America was imposing the ideolexicon "patriotism," their practice consisted in serving foreign interests and their own minority interests, while submitting to exploitation, expropriation and contempt a social majority that was strategically viewed as a collection of minorities.

In Bolivia the indigenous people were always a minority. Minority in the daily newspapers, in the universities, in the majority of Catholic schools, in the public image, in politics, in television. The problem stemmed from the fact that that minority was easily more than half of the invisible population. Somewhat like how today black men and women are called a minority in the southern United States, where they total more than fifty percent. To disguise the fact that the Bolivian ruling class was the ethnic minority of a democratic population, one pretended that an indigenous person, in order to be one, had to wear feathers on their head and speak the Aymara of the 16th century, before the contamination of the colonial period. Since this phenomenon is impossible in any nation and in any moment of history, they were then denied Amerindian citizenship for the sin of impurity. For that, the best resource now consists of systematic mockery in well-publicized books: they mock those who would claim their Amerindian lineage for speaking Spanish and for doing so over the Internet or on a cellular telephone. By contrast, it is never demanded of a good Frenchman or of a traditional Japanese that they urinate behind an orange tree like in Versailles or that their woman walk behind them with her head lowered. Which is to say, the Amerindian peoples are viewed as out of place except in the museum and in dances for tourists. They have no right to progress, that thing which is not an invention of any developed nation but of Humanity throughout its history.

Bolivia's recent separatist referenda—let's dispense with the euphemism—are part of a long tradition, which demonstrates that the ability to retain the past is not the exclusive property of those who refuse to progress but those who consider themselves the vanguard of civilizing progress.

If medieval (which is to say, pre-humanist) cultures and ideologies used to defend with blood-shot fervor in their political and religious sermons differences of class, of race, and of gender as part of nature or of divine right and now they have changed their discourse, it is not because they have progressed thanks to their own tradition but despite that tradition. They have had no other recourse than to recognize and even try to appropriate ideolexicons like “freedom,” “equality,” “diversity,” “minority rights,” etc. in order to legitimate and extend a contrary practice. If democracy was an “invention of the devil” until the mid-20th century, according to this feudal mentality, today not even the most fascist would be capable of declaring it in a public square. On the contrary, their method consists of repeating this word in association with contrary muscular practices until it is emptied of meaning.

It is easy to distinguish between fascist and humanist patriotism or nationalism: one imposes its muscular power and the other claims the right to equality. But since we only have one word and within it are mixed all of the historical circumstances, we usually condemn or praise indiscriminately.

Now, the muscular power of the oppressor is not sufficient; the moral defect of the oppressed is also necessary. Not long ago a Miss Bolivia—with some traces of indigenous features—complained that her country was recognized for its *cholas* (indigenous women) when in reality there were other parts of the country where the women were prettier. This is the same mentality as an impure man named Domingo Sarmiento in the 19th century and most of the educators of the period.

Military colonialism has given way to political colonialism and the latter has passed the baton to cultural colonialism. This is why a government composed of ethnic groups historically repudiated at home and abroad not only must contend with the practical difficulties of a world dominated by and made to order for the capitalist system, whose only flag is the interest and benefit of financial classes, but also must struggle with centuries of prejudice, racism, sexism and classism that are encrusted beneath every pore of the skin of every inhabitant of this slumbering America.

As a reaction to this reality, those who oppose it take recourse to the same method of elevating to power the *caudillos*, individual men or women who must be defended vigorously. From the point of view of humanist analysis, this is a mistake. However, if we consider that the progress of history—when it is possible—is also moved by political changes, then one would have to recognize that the theory of the intellectual must make concessions to the practice of the politician. Nevertheless, again, even though we might suspend this caveat, we must not forget that no humanist progress comes from struggling eternally with the instruments of an old, oppressive and anti-humanist tradition.

But first things first: Bolivia cannot be divided in two based on one rich and white Bolivia and another Indian and poor Bolivia. What moral foundation can a country or an autonomous region have based on acute mental and historical retardation? Why were these separatist—or "decentralized union"—boundaries not arrived at when the government and society were dominated by the traditional Creole classes? Why was it then more patriotic to have a united Bolivia without autonomous indigenous regions?

(2008)

BRAZIL: THE ETERNAL COUNTRY OF THE FUTURE TRAPPED IN ITS COLONIAL PAST

Days before the elections in Brazil, a young Brazilian approached me and said, "God willing, Bolsonaro to win. He is a military man and will end corruption." I did not want to answer. I esteem this boy as a good person, maybe too young to be anything else. But these two brief sentences summed up several volumes of Latin American history to its present.

Beginning with the obvious: if there were governments and corrupt regimes on the continent, those were the military regimes. First, because every dictatorship is corrupt by definition, and second, because direct robberies were always massive, by denouncing the disappearances, then only to reappear by floating in a river with evidence of torture. It would suffice to mention the most recent investigation into the fortune of General Pinochet, a military leader who accumulated several million dollars in salary as an unelected president, without mention of such details as the thousands killed and many more persecuted during his rule. There were shams of decorated honors for assuming "moral reserve" and for the "bastion of courage" by owning weapons financed by the people's work, only to later be threatened by their own armies in "bringing order," by garrison and cemeteries. That same barbaric culture of innumerable generals, soldiers, and scoundrels boasting to be "macho" and valiant fighters, never won or went to any war against other armies, but dedicated themselves to serving the rural oligarchy by terrorizing and threatening their own people. In the coining of a neologism, millions of thugs are now hidden within their new condition of digital *cowangry*.

This military mentality applied to civil practice and domestic life (deviates from any *raison d'être* of an army) is a Latin American tradition born prior to the Cold War and long before the new republics were born and consolidated with corruption, deep in hypocritical racism. This is especially true in Brazil, the last country in the continent to abolish slavery. Even Captain Bolsonaro's vice presidential candidate, General Mourão, a mulatto man like most of his compatriots, is pleased that his grandson contributes to the "*branqueamento da raça* (whitening of the race)." Have any of us ever crossed paths with this kind of deep racial and social disregard for 90 percent of their own family? The same historical problems permeate in other regions that stand out for their brutality in Central America and the Caribbean.

The second, and less obvious, is the appeal to God. In the same way that the United States replaced Great Britain in its consolidation of Spanish colonial verticality, the Protestant churches did the same with those ultraconservative societies (limitless landowners and silent masses of obedient poor), which had been shaped by the previous hierarchy of the Catholic church. It took some Protestant sects like the Pentecostals and others at least a century more than the dollar and the cannons. The phenomenon probably started in the Sixties and Seventies: those innocent, presumably apolitical, gentlemen, who went door to door talking about God, should have a clear political translation. The paradoxical effect of Christian love (that radical love of Jesus, a rebel who was surrounded by poor and marginal people of all kinds, who did not believe in the chances of the rich reaching heaven, and did not recommend taking the sword but turning the other cheek, who broke several biblical laws such as the obligation to kill adulteresses with stones, who was executed as a political criminal) ended up leading to the hatred of gays and the poor, in the desire to fix everything with shots. Such is the case of medieval candidates like Captain Jair Messias Bolsonaro and many others throughout Latin America, who are supported by a strong and decisive evangelical vote. These people in a trance are watered in sweat and hysterical cries and say they "speak in tongues," but just speak their disjointed language of political and social hatred in blind fanaticism that God prefers them with a gun in their hands rather than peaceably fighting for justice, respect for the different, and against arbitrary powers.

In the midst of the euphoric golden decade of progressive governments, such as Lula's, we note two mistakes: naive optimism and the dangers of corruption, and the ramifications of a domino effect because corruption was not a creation of any government, but instead a mark of identity of the Brazilian culture. To name just one more case, this is also the state of affairs in neighboring Argentina.

We must add to all this that the traditional social narrators of a more rancid and powerful Latin America can be found in Maduro's Venezuela where the equally pathetic opposition is never mentioned. As the example, this is the perfect excuse to continue terrorizing about something that almost all the countries of the continent have lived with since the colony: poverty, economic crises, dispossession, impunity, civil and military violence. So it is Venezuela that is exemplifying Brazilian propaganda and not the Brazil of Lula that took 30 million out of poverty, the one with super entrepreneurs, the one of "Deus é brasileiro (God is Brazilian)," the Brazil that was going away to eat the world and had passed the GDP of U.K.

It was the perfect alibi: for others to believe that corruption did not have 200 years of brutal exercise but had been created by the last five to 10 years of a pair of leftist governments. On the contrary, these governments were an ideological exception within a deeply conservative, racist, classist, and sexist continent. Everything that now finds resonance from Europe to Latin America, to the United States, abandons the ideals of Enlightenment and plunges neurotically into a new Middle Ages.

We still don’t know whether this medieval reaction of the traditional forces in power is just that; a reaction, or a long historical tendency of several generations that began in the Eighties and stumbled 15 years ago.

For the second round in Brazil, the coalition against Bolsonaro has already launched the slogan: "Juntos pelo Brasil do diálogo e do respeito (Together for Brazil for dialogue and respect)." This motto only goes to show that those who oppose Bolsonaro in Brazil, like those who oppose Trump in the United States, do not understand the new *cowangry* mentality. The *cowangry* need to know that there is someone else (not them) who is going to return women to the kitchens, gays to their closets, blacks to work on the plantations, and poor to the industries, that someone is going to throw a bomb in some favela ("dead the dog, dead to the rage"). Someone will torture all who think differently (especially poor blacks, teachers, journalists, feminists, critics, educated people without titles, and other dangerous subversives with foreign ideas, all in the name of God) and in that way, someone will punish and exterminate all those miserable people solely responsible for the personal frustrations of the *cowangry*.

(2018)

The Fragments of the Latin American Union

In Latin America, in the absence of a social revolution at the moment of national independence there were plenty of rebellions and political revolts. Less frequently these were popular rebellions and almost never were they ideological revolutions that shook the traditional structures, as was the case with the North American Revolution, the French Revolution, and the Cuban Revolution. Instead, internal struggles abounded, before and after the birth of the new Republics.

A half century later, in 1866, the Ecuadorian Juan Montalvo would make a dramatic diagnosis: "freedom and fatherland in Latin America are the sheep's clothing with which the wolf disguises himself." When the republics were not at war they enjoyed the peace of the oppressors. Even though slavery had been abolished in the new republics, it existed *de facto* and was almost as brutal as in the giant to the north. Class violence was also racial violence: indigenous people continued to be marginalized and exploited. "This has been the peace of the jail cell," concluded Montalvo. The Indian, deformed by this physical and moral violence, would receive the most brutal physical punishments but "when they give him the whip, trembling on the ground, he gets up thanking his tormenter: *May God reward you, sir*." Meanwhile, the Puerto Rican Eligenio M. Hostos in 1870 would already lament "there is still no South American Confederation." On the contrary, he only saw disunion and new empires oppressing and threatening: "An empire [Germany] can still move deliberately against Mexico! Another empire [Great Britain/Brazil] can still wreck Paraguay with impunity!"

But the monolithic admiration for Europe, like that of Sarmiento, also begins to fall apart at the end of the 19th century: "Europe is no happier and has nothing to throw in our face with regard to calamities and misfortunes" (Montalvo). "The most civilized nations—Montalvo continues—, those whose intelligence has reached the sky itself and whose practices walk in step with morality, do not renounce war: their breasts are always burning, their jealous hearts leap with the drive for extermination." The Paraguay massacre results from muscular reasoning within the continent, and another American empire of the period is no exception to this way of seeing: "Brazil trades in human flesh, buying and selling slaves, in order to bow to its adversary and provide its share of the rationale." The old accusation of imperial Spain is now launched against the other colonialist forces of the period. France and England—and by extension Germany and Russia—are seen as hypocrites in their discourse: "the one has armies for subjugating the world, and only in this way believes in peace; the other extends itself over the seas, takes control of the straits, dominates the most important fortresses on earth, and only in this way believes in peace." In 1883, he also points out the ethical contradictions of the United States, "where the customs counteract the laws; where the latter call the blacks to the Senate, and the former drive them out of the restaurants." (Montalvo himself avoids passing through the United States on his trip to Europe out of "fear of being treated like a Brazilian, and that resentment might instill hatred in my breast," since "in the most democratic country in the world it is necessary to be thoroughly blonde in order to be a legitimate person.")

Nonetheless, even though practice always tends to contradict ethical principles—it is not by accident that the most basic moral laws are always prohibitions—the unstoppable wave of humanist utopia continued to be imposed step by step, like the principle of union in equality, or the "fusion of the races in one civilization." Ibero-American history itself is understood in this universal process "to unite all the races in labor, in liberty, in equality and in justice." When the union is achieved, "then the continent will be called Colombia" (Hostos). For José Martí as well, history was directed inevitably toward union. In "La América" (1883) he foresaw a "new accommodation of the national forces of the world, always in movement, and now accelerated, the necessary and majestic grouping of all the members of the American national family." The union of nations passes from utopia, project of European humanism, to a Latin American commonplace: the fusion of the races in a kind of perfect *mestizaje*. Having rejected the empires of Europe and the United States for such a project, the New World would be "the oven where all the races must be melted, where they are being melted" (Hostos). In 1891, an optimistic Martí writes in New York that in Cuba "there is no race hatred because there are no races" even though this is more of an aspiration than a reality. During the period advertisements were still published in the daily newspapers selling slaves alongside horses and other domesticated animals.

In any case, this relationship between oppressors and oppressed cannot be reduced to Europeans and Amerindians. The indigenous people of the Andes, for example, also had spent their days scratching at the earth in search of gold to pay tribute to those sent by the Inca and numerous Mesoamerican tribes had to suffer the oppression of the Aztec empire. During most of the life of the Ibero-American republics, the abuse of class, race and sex was part of the organization of society. International logic is reproduced in the domestic dynamic. To put it in the words of the Bolivian Alcides Arguedas in 1909, "when a boss has two or more *pongos* [unsalaried workers], he keeps one and rents out the others, as if it were simply a matter of a horse or a dog, with the small difference that the dog and the horse are lodged in a wood hut or in a stable and both are fed; the *pongo* is left to sleep in the doorway and to feed on scraps." Meanwhile the soldiers would take the Indians by the hair and beating them with their sabers carry them off to clean the barracks or would steal their sheep in order to maintain an army troop as it passed through. In the face of these realities, utopian humanists seemed like frauds. Frantz Tamayo, in 1910 declares, "imagine for a moment the Roman empire or the British empire having national altruism as its foundation and as its ideal. [...] Altruism! Truth! Justice! Who practices these with Bolivia? Speak of altruism in England, the country of wise conquest, and in the United States, the country of the voracious monopolies!" According to Angel Rama (1982), modernization was also exercised principally "through a rigid hierarchical system." That is to say, it was a process similar to that of the Conquest and the Independence. In order to legitimate the system, "an aristocratic pattern was applied which has been the most vigorous shaper of Latin American cultures throughout their history."

Was our history really any different from these calamities during the military dictatorships of the end of the 20th century? Now, does this mean that we are condemned by a past that repeats itself periodically as if it were a novelty each time?

Let us respond with a different problem. The popular psychoanalytic tradition of the 20th century made us believe that the individual is always, in some way and in some degree, hostage to a past. Less rooted in popular consciousness, the French existentialists reacted by proposing that in reality we are condemned to be free. That is, in each moment we have to choose, there is no other way. In my opinion, both dimensions are possible in a human being: on the one hand we are conditioned by a past but not determined by it. But if we pay paranoid tribute to that past believing that all of our present and our future is owed to those traumas, we are reproducing a cultural illness: "I am unhappy because my parents are to blame." Or, "I can't be happy because my husband oppressed me." But where is the sense of freedom and of responsibility? Why is it not better to say that "I have not been happy or I have these problems because, above all, I myself have not taken responsibility for my problems"? Thus arises the idea of the passive victim and instead of fighting in a principled way against evils like machismo one turns to the crutch in order to justify why this woman or that other one has been unhappy. "Am I sick? The fault is with the machismo of this society." Etc.

Perhaps it goes without saying that being human is neither only biology nor only psychology: we are constructed by a history, the history of humanity that *creates* us as subjects. The individual—the nation—can recognize the influence of context and of their history and at the same time their own freedom as potential which, no matter how minimal and conditioned it might be, is capable of radically changing the course of a life. Which is to say, an individual, a nation that would reject outright any representation of itself as a victim, as a potted plant or as a flag waved by the wind.

(2004)

Respect Without Rights: The Privatization of Morality

Despite the violent reactions of the owners of the world, the humanist wave that radicalizes recognition of fundamental equality among human beings will not stop. But the price paid in the last seven centuries has been very high. Like any change in values, even when aimed at the center of the humanist paradigm (in part accepted by conservative discourse, very much despite itself), it must necessarily be considered "immoral."

Just one example.

The very definition of "marriage between two people of the same sex" hides a preconceived idea: if the body possesses a penis and testicles, it is a man; if it possesses a vagina and ovaries it is a woman. Biological sex is identified with gender. We know that gender is a cultural construction; there is nothing biological about the fact that little girls are dressed in pink and boys in sky blue or that teenaged girls would die to look and act like a barbie doll while their brother is out looking for a scar or a prostitute to confirm his manhood.

Paradoxically, it is understood that in order to be a "man" or "woman" it is not enough to possess a virile member or a reproductive womb: it is necessary, first of all, "to behave like" such, according to the *naturalized* formulas. At the same time, in order to confer the category of sin upon a sexuality different from our own (supposing that all of us heterosexuals practice sex in the same manner), it is alleged that that person has chosen to be that way. To respond to this accusation, the partisans of gay rights allege that their sexual condition is not rooted in a choice but in an innate, genetic fact. The most frequently repeated argument in support of this idea is formulated as a rhetorical question: "Have heterosexuals chosen their heterosexuality?" A new paradox is derived from this argument: in order to defend a right to freedom, freedom is annulled as a legitimating principle

Now, although we can accept two antagonistic categories, nature and culture, we must observe how both concepts are manipulated to the benefit of one sector or another. For example, the ability to give birth (in Spanish "dar a luz," to bring to light, one of the more beautiful metaphors) belongs to women, and therefore we could define it as a "natural faculty." The problem arises when that faculty is interpreted by other members of society according to their own *values*, which is to say, according to their own *interests*. Thus arise feminine *roles* that have never been dictated by nature but by social power

Recently, a legislator from my country repeated on the radio a well-known rationale. 1) He supported the right of lesbians and homosexuals to "be different." 2) For this reason, he would not vote in favor of legislation that attempted to extend to them the same legal rights we heterosexuals enjoy because 3) he was in favor of the defense of family and values. 4) The defense of heterosexuality is the defense of nature, he concluded

We should observe that to allege a *defense of values*, without specifying to which values one refers, constitutes a new ideolexicon. The implication is that it is possible not to possess or not to be in favor of "values." Nevertheless, nobody lacks a determinate system of values. Even criminals and even more so organized crime are based on a determinate system of values. Very traditional values, if we review the history of crime, whether private, religious or governmental.

We can say the same when the noun *values* is made more precise with the adjective *family*: "we defend family values." But, which family? "The traditional family," comes the response, supposing an absolute, ahistorical, natural category. And to which tradition does one refer? In the face of this kind of questioning, there is a quick retreat to safe ground: the Holy Scriptures. I say "safe" for social reasons, not because of its theological implications, since from the latter point of view there is nothing less unanimous than interpretations of the sacred books.

If the defense is of "the values of the traditional family," we might understand that the speaker is in favor of the oppression of women, of the denial of interracial marriage, interreligious marriage, etc. But I do not believe that many people support this position, since this kind of "traditional values" has been defeated in the historical struggle in favor of a secular (not necessarily irreligious) humanism. Because if many present-day religions defend gender and racial equality (and although primitive Christianity also did so to a radical and revolutionary degree for its time), a millenarian history demonstrates the contrary. We owe to progressive humanism and not to "traditional values" those principles of which even the most reactionary among us now boast.

When one assumes that the prescription of heterosexuality is a defense of nature in order to deny marriage rights to people "of the same sex" there is no explanation of why homosexuals (almost) always came from heterosexual families. Even more curious: in the need to legitimate the denial of others' rights, a Catholic priest praised the Uruguayan legislator for defending nature. This demonstrates the immersion of the priest in the humanist paradigm. It would have been more logical and traditional to take recourse to the will of God (assuming that anyone can arrogate to himself this right) or some Mosaic law, like those that Jesus used to revoke. Since it is recognized that the State of an open society should be secular, one recurs to the paradigms of humanism. But, how does one speak of *natural* when we are talking about the least natural animal of all species? What is natural about the celibate man, sexual abstention or the wearing of skirts in the style of the Middle Ages?

Yes, at least the Catholic Church has a long tradition of recognizing faults and errors. Which is a virtue and the humanist recognition that ideas like the "Papal infallibility" decreed by the

Vatican was an authoritarian fantasy. The problem lies in the fact that those who hold traditional power recognize their errors a hundred years later, when it no longer matters to the victims. As if errors were always in the past and never in the present. As if repentance were part of the strategy of that power in the face of the rise of contrary values.

Since when can a right I possess be perceived as threatened because a peer demands it in the same measure? Or is it that that peer is a peer but not as much of a human being as I because he arrived later in the world? What right do some of us equals have to organize a State in order to exclude other equals at the same time that we brag about the diversity of our societies? Why do we believe we are doing others a favor by *tolerating them*, instead of recognizing that they are the ones doing us a favor by not rebelling violently in order to finally claim those rights that we deny them?

Because the right to be different does not consist of having different rights but, simply, the same rights.

(2007)

Honduras Against History

The Bible relates the story of how the teachers of the law brought before Jesus an adulterous woman. They intended to stone her to death, as they were required to do by the law of God, which at the time was said to be the law of men as well. The teachers and Pharisees wanted to test Jesus, from which one can induce that Jesus was already well known for his lack of orthodoxy with respect to the most ancient laws. Jesus suggested that whoever was free of sin should cast the first stone. Thus nobody was able to execute the strict law.

In this way, and in many others, the Bible itself has continued to be transformed, despite being a collection of books inspired by God. Religions have always been considered to be great conservative forces which, faced with reformers, became great reactionary forces. The paradox is rooted in the fact that all religion, all sects, have been founded by some subversive, by some rebel or revolutionary. It is not for nothing that history teems with those martyred, persecuted, tortured and assassinated by the political powers of the moment.

The men who were persecuting the adulteress retreated, recognizing in the turn of events their own sins. But over the course of history the result has been different. The men who oppress, kill and assassinate the alleged sinners always do so with the justification of some law, some right and in the name of some morality. This, more universal, rule was the one applied in Jesus's own execution. In his time, he was not the only rebel who fought against the Roman Empire. Not coincidentally, he was crucified together with two other prisoners. By association, this was intended to signify that he was just another prisoner being executed. Not even a religious dissident. Not even a political dissident. Invoking other laws, they eliminated the subversive who had questioned the Pax Romana and the collaborationism of the aristocracy and of the religious hierarchies of his own people. Everything was carried out according to the laws. But history recognizes them today by their methods.

George Bush's government gave us plenty of examples, and on a large scale. All of the wars and violations of national and international law were committed in defense of the law and sovereign right. By its sectarian interests, history will judge it. By its methods, its interests shall be known.

In Latin America, the role of the Catholic Church has almost always been the role of the Pharisees and the teachers of the law who condemned Jesus in defense of the dominant classes. There has never been a military dictatorship of oligarchical origin that didn't receive the blessing of bishops and influential priests, thereby legitimizing the censorship, the oppression, the mass murder of the supposed sinners. Now, in the 21st century, the method and the discourses are repeated in Honduras like a crack of the whip from the past.

By their methods we know them. The patriotic discourse, the complacency of an upper class trained in the domination of the poor who have no formal education. A class that owns the methods of popular education, which is what the main communication media are. Censorship; the use of the army to carry out their plans; the repression of mass demonstrations; the expulsion of journalists; the expulsion by force of a government elected by democratic vote, its later demand that Interpol detain him, its threat to jail dissidents if they return and its later denial by force of their return.

In order to better see this reactionary phenomenon let's divide human history into four grand periods:

1) The collective power of the tribe concentrated in one strong member of a family, generally a man.

2) A period of agricultural expansion unified by a totem (something akin to a conquering surname) and later a pharaoh or emperor. During this time wars emerge and primitive armies are consolidated, not so much for the purpose of defense as for the conquest of new productive territories and for state administration of its own people's surplus production and the oppression of its people's slaves. This stage continues with variations up until the absolutist kings of Europe, passing through the feudal era. In

all of these regimes, religion is a central element of cohesion alongside coercion.

3) In the modern era we have a renaissance and a radicalization of the Greek experiment in representative democracy. But in the modern period humanist thought includes the idea of universality, of the implicit equality of every human being, the idea of history as a process of reaching toward perfection instead of inevitable corruption, and the concept of morality as a human product relative to a determined historical time. And perhaps the most important idea, from the Arab philosopher Averroes: political power not as the pure will of God but as the result of social interests, class interests, etc. Liberalism and Marxism are two radicalizations (opposed in their means) of this same current of thought, which also includes Charles Darwin's theory of evolution. This period of representative democracy was the most practical form for bringing together the voices of millions of men and women in one house, the Congress or Parliament. If Humanism pre-exists the techniques for popularizing culture, it is also empowered by them. The printing press, the paperback book, the low-price newspapers of the 19th century, the necessary literacy training of future workers were decisive steps toward democratization. Nonetheless, at the same time the reactionary forces, the dominant forces of the previous period, rapidly conquered these media. Thus, if it was no longer possible to further delay the arrival of representative democracy, it was possible to dominate its instruments. The medieval sermons in the churches, functional in

great measure for the princes and dukes, were reformulated in the media of information and in the media of the new popular culture, like radio, film and television.

4) Despite this, the democratic wave continued on, frequently bathed in blood by successive reactionary coups. In the 21st century the renaissance humanist wave continues. And with it continue the instruments to make it possible. Like the Internet, for example. But so too the contrary forces, the reactions of the powers constituted by the previous stages. And in the process of struggle they learn to use and dominate the new instruments. While *representative democracy* has not yet matured, already one sees emerging the ideas and instruments necessary for passing on to a stage of *direct democracy*, participatory and radical.

In some countries, like today in Honduras, the reaction is not against this latest stage but the previous one. A kind of late reaction. Even though in appearance it suggests a smaller scale, it has Latin American and universal significance. First because it represents a calling to attention of the recent democratic complacency of the continent; and second because it stimulates the *modus operandi* of those reactionaries who have always sailed against the currents of history.

Earlier we noted why the deposed president of Honduras had not violated the law or the constitution. Now we can see that his proposal of a non-binding popular referendum was a method of transition from a *representative democracy* toward a *direct democracy*. Those who interrupted this process reversed it toward the prior stage.

The fourth stage is intolerable for a Banana republic mentality that can be recognized by its methods.

(2009)

The Illegitimate Constitution

The dialectical dispute over the legality of the violent removal from office and expulsion from the country of the president of Honduras has not reached closure. Months ago, I explained my point of view, which is that there was no violation of the constitution on the part of president Zelaya when he called for a non-binding poll on the question of a constituent assembly. But at base this discussion is moot and rooted in a different problem: resistance by a social class and mind-set that formed the estates of its own Banana Republic and seeks desperately to identify any kind of change with chaos, at the same time that it imposes repression on its people and on any adversarial communication media.

The main argument of the authors of the coup in Honduras is rooted in the fact that the 1982 Constitution does not allow changes in its wording (articles 239 and 374) and establishes the removal from power of those who promote such changes. The Law of Citizen Participation of 2006, which promotes popular referenda, was never accused of being unconstitutional. On the contrary, popular participation is prescribed by the very same constitution (article 45). All of which reveals the scholastic spirit of its drafters, nuanced with a humanistic language.

No norm, no law can stand above a country's constitution. Nonetheless, no modern constitution has been dictated by God, but by human beings for their own benefit. Which is to say, no constitution can stand above a natural right like a people's freedom to seek change.

A constitution that establishes its own immutability confuses its precarious human origins with a divine origin; or attempts to establish the dictatorship of one generation over all generations to come. If this principle of immutability made any sense, we would have to suppose that before the constitution of Honduras could be modified Honduras must first disappear as a country. Otherwise, for a thousand years that country would have to be ruled by the same wording.

The orthodox religious have tried to avoid changes in the Koran and in the Bible by counting the number of words. When societies and their values change but a sacred text cannot be altered, the text is salvaged by interpreting it in favor of the new values. This is clearly demonstrated by the proliferation of sects, isms and new religions that arise from the same text. But in a sacred text the prohibition against change, even though impossible, is more easily justified, since no man can amend God's word.

These pretensions of eternity and perfection were not rare in the Ibero-American constitutions that in the 19th century attempted to invent republics, instead of allowing the people to invent their own republics and constitutions to their own measure and according to the pulse of history. If in the United States the constitution of 1787 is still in force, it is due to its great flexibility and its many amendments. Otherwise, this country would have today three fifths of a man in the presidency, a quasi-human. "That ignorant little black man," as the now former de facto Honduran foreign minister Enrique Ortez Colindres called him. As if that weren't enough, article I of the famous constitution of the United States originally prohibited any change in constitutional status with reference to slaves.

The result of a constitution like that of Honduras is none other than its own death, preceded sooner or later by the spilling of blood. Those who claim to defend it will have to do so with force of arms and with the narrow logic of a set of norms that violate one of the most basic and undeniable natural rights.

For centuries, the philosophers who imagined and articulated the utopias that today are called Democracy, State and Human Rights said so explicitly: no law exists above these natural rights. And if such a thing were attempted, disobedience is justified. Violence does not originate from disobedience but from he who violates a fundamental right. Politics is for everything else. Negotiation is the concession of the weak. A convenient concession, inevitable, but in the long term always insufficient.

A mature democracy implies a culture and an institutional system that prevent breaks from the rules of the game. But at the same time, and for that same reason, a democracy is defined by allowing and facilitating the inevitable changes that come with a new generation, with the increased historical consciousness of a society.

A constitution that impedes change is illegitimate in the face of the inalienable right to freedom (to change) and equality (to determine change). Such a constitution is mere paper, it is a fraudulent contract that one generation imposes upon another in the name of a nation that no longer exists.

(2009)

The Devils of Haiti

After Haiti's great earthquake, several theories appeared about the causes. According to Haiti's consul in Brazil, George Samuel Antoine, the fault lay with *macumba,* or African spiritism, and the race: "The African himself is damned. Every place where there are Africans is screwed." ["*O africano em si tem maldição. Todo lugar que tem africano tá foda.*"]

The influential televangelist Pat Robertson asserted that the misfortune was owed to the fact that the Haitian people had a pact with the devil. A secret pact. Perhaps so secret that, with the exception of Pat Robertson, not even God knew about it. Otherwise the infinite love of the Creator would certainly have averted the deaths of thousands of innocent children as a result of this cosmic plot. Or he knew about it and allowed it to happen, not out of weakness but due to his well-known policy of non-intervention.

Another theory, widely held and distributed by thousands of editors, bloggers, and presidents like Hugo Chávez states that the earthquake that wiped the country's capital off the map and killed more than a hundred thousand people was caused by the United States in order to destabilize the regime in Iran. Which demonstrates the tremendous technological power of the United States, capable moving the tectonic plates that hold up the oceans and entire countries.

Although secular, the theory retains a lot of the theological tradition according to which God is in the habit of laying waste to entire peoples in order to keep the corner grocer from being unfaithful to his wife.

Other presidents and columnists claim that U.S. aid in reality constitutes an invasion, in order to pillage Haiti's wealth and achieve a strategic position in the Caribbean, close to Cuba. Further evidence that U.S. intelligence agencies are not paying attention, since everyone knows that Haiti is the poorest country in the hemisphere and that Guantánamo is closer to Cuba, so it's possible that the United States will therefore invade Guantánamo as well.

Or one might have to wonder whether this kind of anti-U.S. theory is not itself the product of some perverse U.S. agency. Because there is no better way of discrediting any anti-imperialist critique than with anti-American stupidities.

At this rate, the day will soon arrive when few will believe that Truman was the president who ordered that two nuclear bombs be dropped over Hiroshima and Nagasaki. An action which, thanks to the heroic sacrifice of tens of thousands of innocent children, probably avoided the death of tens of thousands of innocent children.

While every ideological group makes the argumentative most of Haiti's earthquake, thousands of children continue to suffer and die hopelessly.

But all of our best words are going to die there where a child dies.

All of our best thoughts are going to die there where a child's tears end in hunger, pain and injustice he does not understand.

All of our best ideas and our best speeches become a handful of sterile soil there where a mother places flowers on a small grave.

If any one of our words of horror and of indignation were capable of averting the death of a single child in the world, it would deserve to be a living word. Which is to say, there is no such word.

If our words were to accompany our acts the way joy accompanies a child's smile, the way a country's wealth accompanies the value of its currency, perhaps then our words would have some value.

Our words would then be something more than cowardly symbols, empty speeches, pretty flowers that serve to perfume the bed of the lazy and indignant.

And despite everything, perhaps words still matter when they mobilize. We give them value and meaning when we are moved to act by them.

There, in Haiti, words that move emotionally and do not mobilize are useless.

Let's start by giving something. For those children, a glass of water is worth more than a thousand words.

(2010)

Latin and Latino American Immigration

One of the typical—correction: stereotypical—images of a Mexican has been, for more than a century, a short, drunk, trouble-maker of a man who, when not appearing with guitar in hand singing a *corrido*, was portrayed seated in the street taking a siesta under an enormous sombrero. This image of the perfect idler, of the irrational embodiment of vice, can be traced from old 19th century illustrations to the souvenirs that Mexicans themselves produce to satisfy the tourist industry, passing through, along the way, the comic books and cartoons of Walt Disney and Warner Bros. in the 20th century. We know that nothing is accidental; even the defenders of "innocence" in the arts, of the harmless entertainment value of film, of music and of literature, cannot keep us from pointing out the ethical significance and ideological function of the most infantile characters and the most "neutral" storylines. Of course, art is much more than a mere ideological instrument; but that does not save it from manipulation by one human group for its own benefit and to the detriment of others. Let's at least not reference as "art" that kind of garbage.

Ironies of history: few human groups, like the Mexicans who today live in the U.S.—and, by extension, all the other Hispanic groups—can say that they best represent the spirit of work and sacrifice of this country. Few (North) Americans could compete with those millions of self-abnegating workers who we can see everywhere, sweating beneath the sun on the most suffocating summer days, in the cities and in the fields, pouring hot asphalt or shoveling snow off the roads, risking their lives on towering buildings under construction or while washing the windows of important offices that decide the fate of the millions of people who, in the language of postmodernity, are known as "consumers." Not to mention their female counterparts who do the rest of the hard work—since all the work is equally "dirty"—occupying positions in which we rarely see citizens with full rights. None of which justifies the racist speech that Mexico's president, Vicente Fox, gave recently, declaring that Mexicans in the U.S. do work that "not even black Americans want to do." The Fox administration never retracted the statement, never recognized this "error" but rather, on the contrary, accused the rest of humanity of having "misinterpreted" his words. He then proceeded to invite a couple of "African-American" leaders (someday someone will explain to me in what sense these Americans are African), employing an old tactic: the rebel, the dissident, is neutralized with flowers, the savage beast with music, and the wage slaves with movie theaters and brothels. Certainly, it would have sufficed to avoid the adjective "black" and used "poor" instead. In truth, that kind of semantic cosmetics would have been more intelligent but not completely free of suspicion. Capitalist ethics condemns racism, since capital's productive logic is indifferent to the races and, as the 19th century shows, slave trafficking was always against the interests of industrial production. Hence, anti-racist humanism has a well-established place in the hearts of nations and it is no longer so easy to eradicate it except through practices that hide behind elaborate and persuasive social discourses. Nevertheless, the same capitalist ethics approves the existence of the "poor," and thus nobody would have been scandalized if instead of "blacks," the Mexican president had said "poor Americans." All of this demonstrates, meanwhile, that not only those in the economic North live off of the unhappy immigrants who risk their lives crossing the border, but also the politicians and ruling class of the economic South, who obtain, through millions of remittances, the second most important source of revenue after petroleum, by way of Western Union to the "madre pobre," from the blood and sweat of those expelled by a system that then takes pride in them, and rewards them with such brilliant discourses that serve only to add yet another problem to their desperate lives of fugitive production.

Violence is not only physical; it is also moral. After contributing an invaluable part of the economy of this country and of the countries from which they come—and of those countries from which they were expelled by hunger, unemployment and the disfavor of corruption—the nameless men, the unidentified, must return to their overcrowded rooms for fear of being discovered as illegals. When they become sick, they simply work on, until they are at death's door and go to a hospital where they receive aid and understanding from one morally conscious part of the population while another tries to deny it to them. This latter part includes the various anti-immigrant organizations that, with the pretext of protecting the national borders or defending the rule of law, have promoted hostile laws and attitudes which increasingly deny the human right to health or tranquility to those workers who have fallen into illegality by force of necessity, through the imperial logic of the same system that will not recognize them, a system which translates its contradictions into the dead and destroyed. Of course, we cannot and should not be in favor of any kind of illegality. A democracy is that system where the rules are changed, not broken. But laws are a product of a reality and of a people, they are changed or maintained according to the interests of those who have power to do so, and at times these interests can by-pass the most fundamental Human Rights. Undocumented workers will never have even the most minimal right to participate in any electoral simulacrum, neither here nor on the other side of the border: they have been born out of time and out of place, with the sole function of leaving their blood in the production process, in the maintenance of an order of privilege that repeatedly excludes them and at the same time makes use of them. Everyone knows they exist, everyone knows where they are, everyone knows where they come from and where they're going; but nobody wants to see them. Perhaps their children will cease to be ill-born wage slaves, but by then the slaves will have died. And if there is no heaven, they will have been screwed once and forever. And if there is one and they didn't have time to repeat one hundred times the correct words, they will be worse off still, because they will go to Hell, posthumous recognition instead of attaining the peace and oblivion so desired.

As long as the citizens, those with "true human" status, can enjoy the benefits of having servants in exchange for a minimum wage and practically no rights, threatened day and night by all kinds of haunts, they will see no need to change the laws in order to recognize a reality installed a posteriori. This seems almost logical. Nonetheless, what ceases to be "logical"—if we discard the racist ideology—are the arguments of those who accuse immigrant workers of damaging the country's economy by making use of services like hospitalization. Naturally, these anti-immigrant groups ignore the fact that Social Security takes in the not insignificant sum of seven billion dollars a year from contributions made by illegal immigrants who, if they die before attaining legal status, will never receive a penny of the benefit. Which means fewer guests at the banquet. Nor, apparently, are they able to understand that if a businessman has a fleet of trucks he must set aside a percentage of his profits to repair the wear and tear, malfunctions and accidents arising from their use. It would be strange reasoning, above all for a capitalist businessman, to not send those trucks in for servicing in order to save on maintenance costs; or to send them in and then blame the mechanic for taking advantage of his business. Nevertheless, this is the kind and character of arguments that one reads in the newspapers and hears on television, almost daily, made by these groups of inflamed "patriots" who, despite their claims, don't represent a public that is much more heterogeneous than it appears from the outside—millions of men and women, overlooked by simplistic anti-American rhetoric, feel and act differently, in a more humane way.

Of course, it's not just logical thinking that fails them. They also suffer from memory loss. They have forgotten, all of a sudden, where their grandparents came from. Except, that is, for that extremely reduced ethnic group of American-Americans—I refer to the indigenous peoples who came prior to Columbus and the Mayflower, and who are the only ones never seen in the anti-immigrant groups, since among the xenophobes there is an abundance of Hispanics, not coincidentally recently "naturalized" citizens. The rest of the residents of this country have come from some part of the world other than where they now stand with their dogs, their flags, their jaws outthrust and their hunter's binoculars, safeguarding the borders from the malodorous poor who would do them harm by attacking the purity of their national identity. Suddenly, they forget where a large part of their food and raw materials come from and under what conditions they are produced. Suddenly they forget that they are not alone in this world and that this world does not owe them more than what they owe the world.

Elsewhere I have mentioned the unknown slaves of Africa, who if indeed they are poor on their own are no less unhappy for fault of others; the slaves who provide the world with the finest of chocolates and the most expensive wood without the minimal recompense that the proud market claims as Sacred Law. Strategic fantasy this, which merely serves to mask the one true Law that rules the world: the law of power and interests hidden beneath the robes of morality, liberty and right. I have in my memory, etched with fire, those village youths, broken and sickly, from a remote corner of Mozambique who carried tons of tree trunks for nothing more than a pack of cigarettes. Cargo worth millions that would later appear in the ports to enrich a few white businessmen who came from abroad, while in the forests a few dead were left behind, unimportant, crushed by the trunks and ignored by the law of their own country.

Suddenly they forget or refuse to remember. Let's not ask of them more than what they are capable of. Let's recall briefly, for ourselves, the effect of immigration on history. From pre-history, at each step we will find movements of human beings, not from one valley to another but crossing oceans and entire continents. The "pure race" proclaimed by Hitler had not emerged through spontaneous generation or from some seed planted in the mud of the Black Forest but instead had crossed half of Asia and was surely the result of innumerable cross-breedings and of an inconvenient and denied evolution (uniting blonds with blacks) that lightened originally dark faces and put gold in their hair and emerald in their eyes. After the fall of Constantinople to the Turks, in 1453, the wave of Greeks moving into Italy initiated a great part of that economic and spiritual movement we would later know as the Renaissance. Although generally forgotten, the immigration of Arabs and Jews would also provoke, in the sleepy Europe of the Middle Ages, different social, economic and cultural movements that the immobility of "purity" had prevented for centuries. In fact, the vocation of "purity"—racial, religious and cultural—that sunk the Spanish Empire and led it to bankruptcy several times, despite all of the gold of the Americas, was responsible for the persecution and expulsion of the (Spanish) Jews in 1492 and of the (Spanish) Arabs a century later. An expulsion that, paradoxically, benefited the Netherlands and England in a progressive process that would culminate in the Industrial Revolution. And we can say the same for our Latin American countries. If I were to limit myself to just my own country, Uruguay, I could recall the "golden years"—if there were ever years of such color—of its economic and cultural development, coinciding, not by accident, with a boom in immigration that took effect from the end of the 19th until the middle of the 20th century. Our country not only developed one of the most advanced and democratic educational systems of the period, but also, comparatively, had no cause to envy the progress of the most developed countries of the world, even though its population lacked, due to its scale, the geopolitical weight enjoyed by other countries at the time. At present, cultural immobility has precipitated an inverted migration, from the country of the children and grandchildren of immigrants to the country of the grandparents. The difference is rooted in the fact that the Europeans who fled from hunger and violence found in the Río de la Plata (and in so many other ports of Latin America) the doors wide open; their descendants, or the children and grandchildren of those who opened the doors to them, now enter Europe through the back door, although they appear to fall from the sky. And if indeed it is necessary to remember that a large part of the European population receives them happily, at a personal level, neither the laws nor general practice correspond to this good will. They aren't even third-class citizens; they are nothing and the management reserves the right to deny admission, which may mean a kick in the pants and deportation as criminals.

In order to obscure the old and irreplaceable Law of interests, it is argued—as Oriana Fallaci has done so unjustly—that these are not the times of the First or Second World War and, therefore, one immigration cannot be compared to another. In fact, we know that one period can never be reduced to another, but they can indeed be compared. Or else history and memory serve no purpose. If tomorrow in Europe the same conditions of economic necessity that caused its citizens to emigrate before were to be repeated, they would quickly forget the argument that our times are not comparable to other historical periods and, hence, it's reasonable to forget.

I understand that in a society, unlike a controlled laboratory experiment, every cause is an effect and vice versa—a cause cannot modify a social order without becoming the effect of itself or of something else. For the same reason, I understand that culture (the world of customs and ideas) influences a given economic and material order as much as the other way around. The idea of the determining infrastructure is the basis of the Marxist analytical code, while the inverse (culture as a determinant of socio-economic reality) is basic for those who reacted to materialism's fame. For the reasons mentioned above, I understand that the problem here lies in the idea of "determinism," in either of the two senses. For its part, every culture promotes an interpretive code according to its own Interests and, in fact, does so to the measure of its own Power. A synthesis of the two approaches is also necessary for our problem. If the poverty of Mexico, for example, were only the result of a cultural "deformity"—as currently proposed by the theorists and specialists of Latin American Idiocy—the new economic necessities of Mexican immigrants to the United States would not produce workers who are more stoic and long-suffering than any others in the host country: the result would simply be "immigrant idlers." And reality seems to show us otherwise. Certainly, as Jesus said, "there is none more blind than he who will not see."

(2006)

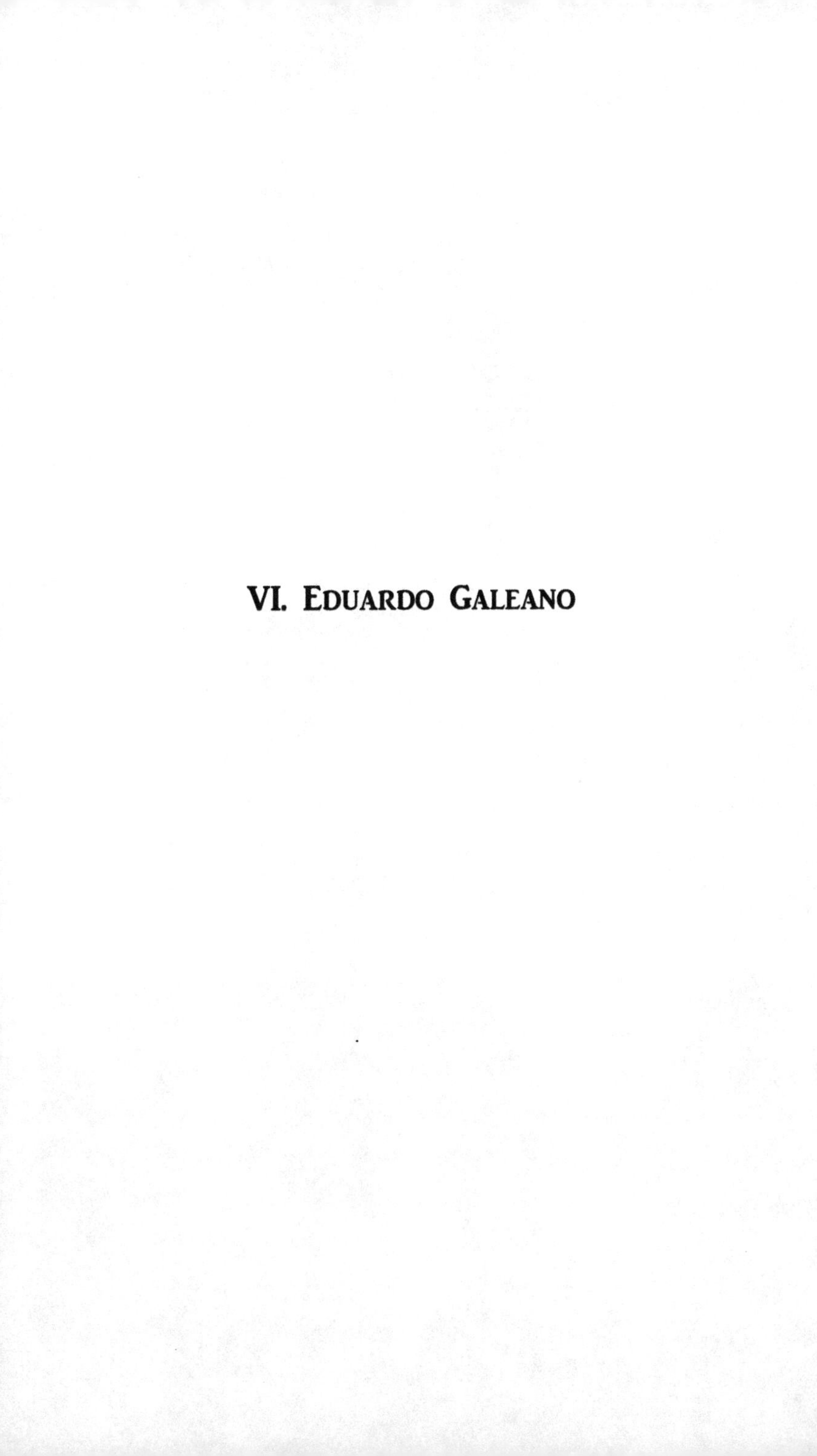

VI. Eduardo Galeano

The Open Eyes of Latin America

There are very few cases of writers who maintain total indifference toward the ethics of their work. There are not so few who have understood that in the practice of literature it is possible to separate ethics from aesthetics. Jorge Luis Borges, not without mastery, practiced a kind of politics of aesthetic neutrality and was perhaps convinced this was possible. Thus, the universalism of Borges' precocious postmodernism was nothing more than the very euro-centrism of the Modern Age nuanced with the exoticism proper to an empire that, much like the British empire, held closely to the old decadent nostalgia for the mysteries of a colonized India and for Arabian nights removed from the dangers of history. It was not recognition of diversity—of freedom in equality—but confirmation of the superiority of the European canon adorned with the souvenirs and booty of war.

Perhaps there was a time in which truth, ethics and aesthetics were one and the same. Perhaps those were the times of myth. This also has been characteristic of what we call engaged literature. Not a literature made for politics but an integral literature, where the text and the author, ethics and aesthetics, go together;

where literature and meta-literature are the same thing. The marketing-oriented thought of postmodernity has been different, strategically fragmented without possible connections. Legitimated by this cultural fad, critics of the establishment dedicated themselves to rejecting any political, ethical or epistemological value for a literary text. For this kind of superstition, the author, the author's context, the author's prejudices and the prejudices of the readers remained outside the pure text, distilled from all human contamination. But, what would remain of a text if we took away from it all of its meta-literary qualities? Why must marble, velvet or sex repeated until devoid of meaning be more literary than eroticism, a social drama or the struggle for historical truth? Rodolfo Walsh said that a typewriter could be a fan or a pistol. Has this fragmentation and later distillation not been a critical strategy for turning writing into an innocent game, into more of a tranquilizer than an instrument of inquiry against the musculature of power?

In his new book, Eduardo Galeano responds to these questions with unmistakable style—Borges would recognize: with benign contempt—without concerning himself with them directly. Like his previous books, starting with *Days and Nights of Love and War (1978)*, *Mirrors* is organized with the postmodern fragmentation of the brief capsule narrative. Nevertheless, the entire book, like the rest of his work, evinces an unbreakable unity. His aesthetics and his ethical convictions as well. Even in the midst of the most violent ideological storms that shook recent history, this ship has not broken up.

Mirrors expands to other continents from the geographical area of Latin America that for decades had been Eduardo Galeano's main interest. His narrative technique is the same as in the trilogy *Memory of Fire* (1982-1986): with an impersonal narrator who fulfills the purpose of approaching the anonymous and plural voice of "the others" and avoiding personal anecdote, at times organized thematically and generally in chronological order, the book begins with the cosmogonic myths and culminates in our times. Each brief text is an ethical reflection, almost always revealing a painful reality and with the invaluable consolation of a beautiful narration. Perhaps the principle of Greek tragedy is none other than this: lesson and turmoil, hope and resignation or the greater lesson of failure. As in his previous books, the paradigm of the engaged Latin American writer, and above all the paradigm of Eduardo Galeano, seems to be reconstructed once again: history can progress, but that ethical-aesthetical progress takes mythical origins as its utopian destination, and memory and awareness of oppression for its instruments. Progress consists of regeneration, of the recreation of humanity in the same manner that the wisest, most just and most vulnerable of the Amerindian gods, the man-god Quetzalcóatl, would have undertaken it.

If we were to remove the ethical code with which each text is read, *Mirrors* would shatter into brilliant fragments; but it would reflect nothing. If we were to remove the aesthetic mastery with which this book was written it would cease to be memorable. Like myths, like the mythical thought redeemed by the author, there is no way of separating one part from the whole without altering the sacred order of the cosmos. Each part is not only an alienated fragment but a tiny object that has been unearthed by a principled archeologist. The tiny object is valuable in its own right, but has even greater value due to the other fragments that have been organized around it, and these latter become even more valuable due to those fragments that have been lost and that are now revealed in the empty spaces that have been formed, revealing an urn, an entire civilization buried by wind and barbarism.

The first law of the narrator, to not be boring, is respected. The first law of the engaged intellectual as well: never does entertainment become a narcotic instead of a lucid aesthetic pleasure.

Mirrors has been published this year simultaneously in Spain, Mexico, and Argentina by Siglo XXI, and in Uruguay by Ediciones del Chanchito. The latter continues an already classic collection of black cover books that has reached number 15, represented meaningfully with the Spanish letter *ñ*. The texts are accompanied with illustrations in the manner of little vignettes that recall the careful art of book publishing in the Renaissance, in addition to the author's drawings as a young man. Even though his conception of the world leads him to think structurally, it is difficult to imagine Eduardo Galeano skipping over any detail. Like a good jeweler of the word who polishes in search of every one of his different reflections, he is equally careful in the publication of his books as works of art. The English edition, *Mirrors, Stories of Almost Everyone*, translated by Mark Fried, will be published by Nation Books.

With each new contribution, this icon of Latin American literature confirms for us that additional formal prizes, like the Cervantes Prize, should not be long in coming.

(2009)

"The Hoariest of Latin American Conspiracy Theorists"

Although I would say that the article "The Land of Too Many Summits" by Christopher Sabatini (*Foreign Affairs*, April 12, 2012) is right on some points, it nonetheless fails to give little more than unproved opinions on other matters—or as Karl Popper would say, certain statements lack the "refutability" condition of any scientific statement—and is inaccurate in terms of its overall meaning.

For years I have argued that Latin American victimhood and the habit of blaming "the Empire" for everything that is wrong is a way to avoid taking responsibility for one's own destiny. Mr. Sabatini is probably right in the central point of his article: "If the number of summits were a measure of the quality of diplomacy, Latin America would be a utopia of harmony, cooperation, and understanding." However, Latin American leaders continue to practice antiquated traditions founded upon an opposing ideology: a certain cult of personality, the love for perpetual leadership positions, the abuse of grandiloquent words and promises, and the sluggishness of concrete and pragmatic actions and reforms, all of which are highly ironic features of governments that consider themselves "progressive." Regardless, not all that long ago, when conservative dictatorships or marionette governments in some banana republic or another manifested such regressive characteristics, it didn't seem to bother the leaders of the world's wealthiest populations all that much.

On some other basic points, Sabatini demonstrates factual inaccuracies. For example, when he states that Eduardo Galeano "wrote the classic screed against the developed world's exploitation and the region's victimhood, *Open Veins of Latin America*, read by every undergraduate student of Latin America in the 1970s and 1980s," he forgets—I cannot assume any kind of intellectual dishonesty since I don't know much about him, but neither can I accuse him of ignorance, since he has followed "Latin American politics for a living"—that at that time Latin America was not the magic-realist land of colorful communist dictators (with the exception of Cuba) as many Anglo readers frequently assume, but rather the land of brutal, conservative, right-wing military dictatorships with a very long history.

Therefore—anyone can logically infer the true facts—that famous book was broadly forbidden in that continent at that time. Of course, in and of itself, the widespread prohibition against it made the publication even more popular year after year. But such popularity did not primarily stem from the book's portrayal of the self-victimization of an entire continent—which I am not going to totally deny—but was more in response to Galeano's frank representation of another reality, not the false imaginings of certain horrible conspiracy theorists, but rather the reality created throughout Latin American history by other delusional people, some of whom became intoxicated by their access to power, although they themselves did not actually wield it in the formal sense.

Therefore, if Eduardo Galeano—a writer, not a powerful CEO, a commander in chief of some army, another drunken president, nor the leader of some obscure sect or lobby—is "the hoariest of Latin American conspiracy theorists," then who or what is and was the de facto hoariest of Latin American *conspirators*? Forget the fact that Galeano is completely bald and try to answer that question.

Regrettably, it has become commonplace for the mass media and other supporters of the status-quo to ridicule one of the most courageous and skillful writers in postmodern history, and to even label him an idiot. However, if Eduardo Galeano was wrong in his arguments—no one can say he was wrong in his means, because his means have always been words, not weapons or money—at least he was wrong on behalf of the right side, since he chose to side with the weak, the voiceless and the nobodies, those who never profit from power, and consequently, we may argue, always suffer at its hands.

He did not pick white or black pieces from the chessboard, but instead chose to side with the pawns, who historically fought in wars organized by the aristocracy from the rearguard (kings, queens, knights, and bishops). Upon the conclusion of battle, that same aristocracy always received the honors and conquered lands, while the pawns were forever the first to die.

Thus, has it been in modern wars. With the ridiculous but traditional exception of some prince playing at war, real soldiers are mostly from the middle and lower classes. Although a few people have real money and everyone has real blood, as a general rule, only poor people contribute to wars with their blood, whereas only rich people contribute to wars with their money—not so hard to do when one always has abundant material means, and even less difficult when such a monetary contribution is always an interest-bearing investment, whether in terms of actual financial gain or perceived moral rectitude, both of which may well be considered as two sides of the same coin.

Is it mere coincidence that the economically powerful, the politicians in office, the big media owners and a variety of seemingly official self-appointed spokespersons for the status quo are the ones who continuously repeat the same tired litany about the glory of heroism and patriotism? It can hardly be a matter of chance, considering that such individuals have a clear need to maintain high morale among those who are actually going to spill their own blood upon the sacrificial altar of war, and have an equally evident motive for demoralizing to the greatest extent possible those skeptics or critics such as Eduardo Galeano who cross the line, and who never buy those jewels of the Crown.

(2012)

Past, Present, and Future: Interview with Eduardo Galeano

Interview with Eduardo Galeano

I. Past

Jorge Majfud: A humanist vision considers history to be a human product, which is to say, a product of the freedom of its individuals and the diverse groups that have enacted it and interpreted it. An anti-humanist vision asserts that, on the contrary, those individuals and groups are the result of history itself, and their freedom is an illusion. If you allow me to limit the choices artificially within this possible spectrum, where do you situate yourself in it?

Eduardo Galeano: Based on what I have experienced in my life, I have the impression that we make the history that makes us. When the history that we make comes out crooked, or is usurped by the few among us who rule, we blame it on history.

J. M.: In this vision there is no room for materialist determinism or for any kind of religious fatalism. . .

E. G.: Fatalisms are comforting, they allow you to sleep soundly, fate is inscribed in the stars, history moves along by itself, don't be bitter, there's no choice but accept it. Fatalisms lie, because if life is not an adventure in freedom, someone should come and explain to me whether living is worth the trouble. But notice: the enlightened ones lie also, the select few who are attributed the power to change reality by touching it with their magic wand: and if reality does not obey me, it doesn't deserve me.

J. M.: If the time of modern revolutions, that is, of abrupt and violent revolutions has passed, is it evolution or resistance that is the better alternative in our times?

E. G.: Who knows how many worlds there are in the world, and how many times there are in time. History walks with our feet, but sometimes it walks very slowly, and sometimes it seems motionless. At any rate, when the changes come from below, from the lower depths, sooner or later they find their way, at their own pace. From below, I mean, from the foot, like in the Zitarrosa song. The only things made from above are wells.

J. M.: Your latest book *Espejos* (*Mirrors*) represents an effort that is both creative and archeological and covers a vast geographic and temporal space. Which periods of history do you believe would win first prize for cruelty and injustice?

E. G.: There are too many favorites in that championship.

J. M.: Okay, more to the point, could you sum up cruelty in an image, in a situation that you have experienced?

E. G.: It happened to me years ago, in a truck that was crossing the upper Paraná. Except for me, everyone was from that area. Nobody spokes. We were packed closely together, in the bed of the truck, bouncing around. Next to me, a very poor woman, with a baby in her arms. The baby was burning with fever, crying. The woman just said that she needed a doctor, that somewhere there had to be a doctor. And finally, we arrived somewhere, I don't know how many hours had gone by, the baby hadn't cried for a long time. I helped that woman get off the truck. When I picked up the baby, I saw that the baby was dead. The killer who had committed this cruelty was an entire system of power, neither in prison nor traveling around on rickety old trucks.

J. M.: With memories like that, we should stop here. But the world keeps turning. Do you believe that the pre-Colombian past has survived so many years of colonization and modernization, enough to define a Latin American way of being, feeling, and even thinking?

E. G.: For centuries, the gods have come, who knows how, from the American past and from the African jungle and from everywhere. Many of those gods travel with other names and use fake passports, because their religions are called superstitions and they continue to be condemned to the underground.

II. Present

J. M.: Are we witnessing the end of capitalism, of a paradigm based on consumerism and financial success, or is this simply one more crisis which will end up strengthening the system itself, the same hegemonic culture?

E. G.: I frequently receive invitations to attend the burial of capitalism. We know quite well, however, that this system—which privatizes its profits but kindly socializes its losses and, as if that weren't enough, tries to convince us that that is philanthropy—will live more than seven lives. To a great degree, capitalism feeds off the discrediting of its alternatives. The word socialism, for example, has been emptied of meaning, by the bureaucracy that used it in the name of the people and by the social democracy that in its name modernized capitalism's *look*. We know that this capitalist system is managing quite well to survive the catastrophes that it unleashes. We don't know, on the other hand, how many lives its main victim—the planet we inhabit, squeezed to the last drop—will be able to live. Where will we move, when the planet is left without water, without land, without air? The company Lunar International is already selling plots of land on the moon. At the end of 2008, the Russian multimillionaire Roman Abramovich made a gift of a little plot to his fiancée.

J. M.: Perhaps he intends to be the first man to give a piece of the moon to his wife, which turns out to be a kind of romantic capitalism. Do you believe that if China, for example, had a hegemonic economy it would quickly become a new empire, colonialist and dominating like any other empire?

E. G.: If I were a professional prophet, I would die of hunger. I'm not even right in soccer, and that is something I know something about. All I can say to you is what I can see: China is putting into practice a successful combination of political dictatorship, in the old communist style, with an economy that functions at the service of the capitalist world market. China can thus provide an extremely cheap workforce to U.S. enterprises like Walmart, which bans unions.

J. M.: Speaking of which, on the most recent "Black Friday," the one day of the year that large retail chains in the U.S. sell at cost, an avalanche of shoppers couldn't wait for the doors to be opened at one of those Walmart and they ran over an employee. The man was crushed to death... Despite all this absurdity, can we think that humanity finds itself in an improved state of individual rights and collective conscience? What is best about our times?

E. G.: In the 20th century, justice was sacrificed in the name of freedom, and freedom was sacrificed in the name of justice. Our time is now the 21st century, and the best it has to offer is the challenge it presents: it invites us to fight to assist the reunion of freedom and justice. They want to live real close to each other, back to back.

J. M.: Can we compare the appearance of the Internet with the revolution produced by the printing press in the 15th century?

E. G.: I have no idea, but it is important to remember that the printing press was not born in the 15th century. The Chinese had invented it two centuries earlier. In reality, the three inventions that made the Renaissance possible were all Chinese inventions: the printing press, the compass, and gunpowder. I don't know if education has improved today, but before we used to learn a universal history reduced to the history of Europe. From the Middle East, nothing or almost nothing. Not a word about China, nothing about India. And about Africa, we only knew what professor Tarzan taught us, and he was never there. And about the American past, about the pre-Colombian world, some little folkloric thing, a few colored feathers . . . and ciao.

J. M.: What is the greatest danger of technological progress in communication?

E. G.: In communication, and in everything else. Machines are no saints, but they are not to blame for what we do with them. The greatest danger lies in the possibility that the computer can program us, just like the automobile drives us. With frightening ease, we become instruments of our instruments.

J. M.: As a writer and as a reader, what kind of reading occupies most of your time these days?

E. G.: I read everything, starting with the walls that accompany my steps through the streets of the cities.

J. M.: Are cruelty and injustice the greatest provocations for the literature of Eduardo Galeano?

E. G.: No. If that were the case, I would have already fallen ill from unmitigated sadness. Luckily, I am a busybody, curious by birth, and I am always seeking out the third bank of the river, that mysterious place where humor and horror meet.

J. M.: For what do you think our times will be remembered in the centuries to come?

E. G.: Will it be remembered? Will there be centuries to come? May God hear you, and if God is deaf, may the Devil hear you.

III. Future

J. M.: Eduardo, do you believe the world will move in the direction of a greater balance of its geographical, social, and cultural divisions or, on the contrary, are we condemned to repeat the same forms of what we today consider physical and moral violence?

E. G.: Condemned, we are not. Fate is a challenge, although at first sight it might appear to be a curse.

J. M.: Does an improvement of our present lie mainly in the deepening of humanist values from the European tradition or in a revaluation of a lost origin in the "peripheral" nations?

E. G.: The European tradition is not enough. We Americans are the children of many mothers. Europe yes, but there are also other mothers. And not only the Americans. All the little human beings all over the world much more than what they believe they are. But the earthly rainbow will not shine, in all its brilliance, as long is it continues to be mutilated by racism, machismo, militarism, elitism, and all those isms that deny us the fullness of our diversity. And by the way, it is fitting to clarify that the humanist values of the European tradition were developed while Europe was exterminating indigenous people in the Americas and selling human flesh in Africa. John Locke, the philoso-pher of freedom, was a shareholder in a slave-trading company.

J. M.: Yes, not unlike the imperial democracies, from ancient Athens to the United States. But does that mean that history always repeats itself?

E. G.: She doesn't want to repeat herself, she doesn't like that one bit, but very often we oblige her to. To give you a very current example, there are parties who come into the government promising a program of the left and wind up repeating what the right wing did. Why don't they let the right continue doing it, since they have the experience? History grows bored, and democracy is discredited, when we are invited to choose between one and the same.

J. M.: What role do "non-organic" intellectuals fulfill in society today? Do they continue to be, at least a few of them, a critical and provocative force?

E. G.: I believe that writing is not a useless passion. But that generalization, "intellectuals," organic or non-organic, doesn't look much like the real world. It takes all kinds to make the world.

In my case, I can tell you that I work with words, that I am totally useless otherwise, and that is the only thing that I do more or less well, and that it seems to me, based on my own and others' experience, that the act of reading is a secret, and sometimes fertile, ceremony of communion. Anyone who reads something that is really worth the trouble does not read with impunity. Reading one of those books that breathe when you put them to your ear does not leave you untouched: it changes you, even if only a little bit, it integrates something into you, something that you did not know or had not imagined, and it invites you to seek, to ask questions. And more still: sometimes it can even help you to discover the true meaning of words betrayed by the dictionary of our times. What more could a critical consciousness want?

J. M.: But contemporary writers tend to avoid that word, "intellectuals." Why?

E. G.: I will answer for myself, not in the name of "writers," which is also a dubious generalization. I write wanting to speak and express myself in a language that is *sentipensante* (feeling-thinking), a very precise word taught to me by fishermen of the Colombian coast of the Caribbean Sea. And for that reason, precisely for that reason, I don't like at all to be called an intellectual. I feel like I am thereby turned into a bodiless head, which is also an uncomfortable situation, and that my reason and emotion are being divorced from one another. One supposes that an intellectual is someone capable of knowing, but I prefer someone capable of comprehending. A cultured person is not someone who accumulates more knowledge, because then there will be nobody more cultured than a computer. A cultured person is someone who knows how to listen, to listen to others and listen to the thousand and one voices of the natural world of which we are a part. In order to speak, I listen. I write on a round-trip journey, I pick up words that I return, stated in my method and manner, to the world from which they come.

J. M.: Speaking of which, what is your narrative technique, that is, your writing habits and behaviors?

E. G.: I have no schedules. I don't make myself write. In Santiago, Cuba, an old drummer, who played like the gods, taught me: "I play," he told me, "when my hand itches." And I paid attention. If I don't itch, I don't write. In literature, like in soccer, when the pleasure turns into duty, it becomes something pretty similar to slave labor. The books write me, they grow inside me, and every night I fall asleep thanking them, because they allow me to believe that I am the author. And having said this I will point out to you that I write each page many times, that I scratch out, I suppress, I re-write, I tear up, I start over again, and all that is part of the great happiness of feeling that what I say is similar to, and sometimes very similar to, what my pages want to say.

J. M.: Your books after the military dictatorships in Uruguay and Argentina, after exile, are different in style. Or perhaps they deepen one characteristic: your gaze continues being that of a non-conformist rebel, but your voice becomes more lyrical. If I remember correctly, it was Jean-Paul Sartre who said that a writer's technique transmits his conception of the world. How would you define your style? Does it reflect your perception of the world or, perhaps, your aspirations about it, or is style something accidental, a form of doing things that comes from a history of aesthetics, from an influence of the adolescent years?

E. G.: My style is the result of many years of writing and erasing. Juan Rulfo used to tell me, showing me one of those pencils that you now almost never see: "I write with the graphite in the tip, but I write more with the other end, where the eraser is." That is what I do or try to do. I try to always say more with less.

J. M.: One common element of committed literature, of the revolutionary utopias up until the seventies, from the years prior to the dictatorships in South America, seems to be happiness. As an example to illustrate this, we could make an exhibit of photographs of the severe faces of the Pinochets, on one side, and of the smiling faces of the Che Guevaras on the other. Does a connection exist between the "aesthetics of sadness" of the literature of the 20th century and society's conservative forces? To what degree is happiness, the Epicureanism of which Amerigo Vespucci spoke with reference to a certain image of native Americans, subversive?

E. G.: I will return to the Colombian coast, and I will tell you that there, the worst insult is *amargao* (a bitter person). Nothing worse can be said to you. And not without reason, because at the end of the day, there is nothing in the world that doesn't deserve to be laughed at. If the literature of denunciation is not, at the same time, a literature of celebration, it distances itself from life as lived and puts its readers to sleep. Its readers are supposed to burn with indignation, but they are nodding off instead. It often happens that the literature that claims to speak to the people only speaks to those who are already persuaded. Without taking any risks, it seems more like masturbation than the act of love, even though according to what I have been told the act of love is better, because one gets to know people. Contradiction moves history, and the literature that truly stimulates the energy of social change helps us to find the secret suns that every night conceals, that human feat of laughing in the face of all evidence. The Judeo-Christian heritage, which so praises pain, does not help much. If I remember correctly, in the entire Bible not a single laugh is heard. The world is a vale of tears, the ones who suffer the most are the chosen ones who ascend to Heaven.

J. M.: How do you imagine the world in fifty years?

E. G.: At my age, I imagine that in fifty years I will no longer be here. As you can see, I have a prodigious imagination.

J. M.: Onetti once said that he wrote for himself. Would Galeano write if he had the bad fortune to be the sole survivor of a worldwide catastrophe?

E. G.: The sole survivor? Ay! I would die of boredom. Perhaps I would write anyway, because that's my vice, but writing for nobody is worse than dancing with your own sister. Onetti got mad at me one night when I committed a juvenile insolence. He told me that he wrote for himself, and I offered to take his letters to Juan Carlos Onetti, Gonzalo Ramírez Street, Montevideo, etc., etc. to the Post Office. He got pissed off. He got pissed off because he was lying, and he knew it quite well. Anyone who publishes their writing writes for others.

J. M.: What would you do differently if you had the experience and opportunity to do it all over again? What does Eduardo Galeano regret?

E. G.: I have no regrets. I am the sum of all the times I put my foot in my mouth as well.

(2011)

The Open Veins of Eduardo Galeano

On June 2, 2014, *Washington Post* article entitled "Latin Americans Are Embracing Globalization and Their Former Colonial Masters," written by a political science professor from the University of Colorado, the author begins with the following sentence: "Uruguayan writer Eduardo Galeano recently renounced his 1971 classic, *Open Veins of Latin America*, one of a few books admitted into the Latin American left's pantheon." Some days before, the *New York Times* had fired off an article entitled "Eduardo Galeano Disavows His Book *The Open Veins*," etc.

Similar examples abound in several languages, above all in the Spanish-language press. For some days and weeks, gloomy articles and commentaries were popping up. It seemed that we were witnessing, along with the correspond-ding euphoria of conservatives, the suicide of radical Latin American literary criticism. Clearly, too much was being read into all of this.

When I read the first articles about the author's recent statements in Brazil, I had a few words with Galeano himself about them. I never was particularly crazy about that book, and I even wrote a pretty harsh paper on it, but in my view it was nonetheless still one of the most courageous books of its era, if not *the* most. I feel that it is a crime to interpret it out of context, and I never dreamed that its own author might be capable of doing such a thing, as can be inferred from each of the opportunistic articles that followed.

I've never been a communist, nor have I worn a Che-styled beret, nor do I think that dissident Cubans are a bunch of *gusanos* (worms) just because they voice their disagreement and aren't able to do so in their own country. Not all of them are like Posada Carriles. However, every time that someone lets me know that Che Guevara was a cruel guerrilla fighter (the summary executions that took place during the first year of the Cuban Revolution are completely unjustifiable), I take it as one historical fact among many others. It follows that when one classifies him as a *murderer*, one does so by systematically omitting the historical context in which he lived—not only does one sidestep the fact that Che was always at the forefront of his revolutionary adventures against the imperial powers of the moment, not at the rear like powerful men throughout the ages, but one also omits, if not outright ignores, that as a youth Guevara was in Guatemala when the CIA bombed the capital city in 1954 for the purpose of destroying a rare example of Central American democracy, which was afterwards labeled a *dictatorship* by our noble press.

And it continued doing so in a variety of ways, as proven by Boston University professor Stephen Kinzer in his latest book *The Brothers* (about the paranoid Dulles brothers) and proven by thousands of declassified documents available for reading at George Washington University.

So, for the moment I'll set aside some skeptical literary theories that find comfort in stating that only the text matters, not the author. Although the author is no longer the authority on his own text, in this case ideological conclusions and the usual "I told you so" aren't the text—the book—but rather the author's own interpretation. So, this time it does make some sense to turn to the author as a means of interpreting what was said. I present here some passages from different exchanges of correspondence, some of the latest ones that I've had with Galeano, and which I obviously share with his approval.

Jorge: A couple of years ago you told me that it was really hard for you to read *The Open Veins of Latin America*, that it was a book with defects, that the reality at the beginning of this century differed substantially from the reality of the 20th century, etc. I never commented on these opinions because they seemed reasonable to me, almost uninteresting, about a book published thirty-plus years ago, and above all because you shared them with me in a private conversation between two friends. You've said more or less the same thing in Brazil some weeks ago, and since then the big media outlets throughout the world haven't tired of publicizing that one of the top exponents of leftist thought has undergone a process of conversion, like Vargas Llosa but a bit late, that the committed intellectuals of the past century have acknowledged their mistakes, that beyond mistakes it would seem as if the Church were apologizing for the inquisition, as if China were to allow discussion on Tiananmen, and the United States were to acknowledge the tragedies of Vietnam and Iraq. I once also told you that in my opinion *The Open Veins of Latin America* was a book with defects and only a partial look at reality (but what book gives a complete look, aside from *The Aleph* by Borges?), but it was and continues to be a courageous and stirring book.

Eduardo: The dogs are barking, Sancho. It's proof that writing is good for something, at least for inspiring celebration and protest, applause and also indignation. The book, written ages ago, is still alive and kicking. I am simply honest enough to admit that at this point in my life the old writing style seems rather stodgy, and that it's hard for me to recognize myself in it since I now prefer to be increasingly brief and untrammeled. This has nothing whatsoever to do with Vargas Llosa.

Jorge: Don't you think that your otherwise useful self-criticism is being exploited for ideological purposes? Or perhaps we've come to the end of history and we no longer see injustice or exploitation anywhere?

Eduardo: As former Costa Rican president Figueres once managed to remark, "What's going wrong here is everything." Jorge, you can write down whatever you like. I fully believe in your talent and honesty. The other voices that have been raised against me and against *The Open Veins of Latin America* are seriously ill with bad faith.

(2014)

VII. Noam Chomsky

Rescuing Memory. Conversations with Noam Chomsky

JUST BEFORE TWELVE THIRTY on a recent spring afternoon, I found myself on the campus of the Massachusetts Institute of Technology, in the building that houses both the linguistics and philosophy departments. A group of Japanese students, full of youthful excitement, were waiting outside Noam Chomsky's eighth-floor office. They approached the door and read the name card on it. They took pictures—lots of pictures—with happy and surprised expressions, but then quickly turned serious. They paused for a brief moment of silence, which almost felt mystical, and then headed out.

At the age of eighty-seven, the renowned linguist, philosopher, historian, cognitive scientist, and critic Noam Chomsky maintains the same clarity found in any of his books, lectures, or television appearances dating back to the 1970s. While in a face-to-face conversation he might adopt an informal and humorous tone towards relevant topics, he is very much that same serious and detailed thinker we all recognize from the conferences and different interviews—one of those individuals history will remember for centuries.

*Years after having met Chomsky at Princeton University and collaborating with him on the Spanish translation of a book (*Ilusionistas, *2012), I was now interested in finding out the roots of his social and political thinking during our meeting. I started by remembering the many letters we'd exchanged for the better part of a decade. In one of the letters I had commented about how my son was adjusting to a society that was his but only by birth, noting that he spoke English with a slight Spanish accent. When Chomsky had a chance, he wrote me this:*

When I was a boy, we were the only Jewish family in a terribly anti-Semitic neighborhood. Those streets weren't any fun for us but our parents never found that out. In a way, you avoid telling your parents what happened to you during those days.

I reminded him of this in order to start a dialogue about that world and its universal implications. What follows is a conversation that went beyond what was initially planned.

Jorge Majfud: Before World War II, anti-Semitism and Nazism were much more common in the United States than Americans are willing to accept today. Henry Ford (awarded the Grand Cross of the German Eagle by the Nazi Government), General Motors, Alcoa, and Texaco are just a few examples of supportive U.S. business interests. And after the war, Jews faced serious and absurd obstacles in migrating as refugees while many Nazis were granted visas (through Mexico) to help develop NASA programs. What memories do you have of those times when you were a Jewish teenager?

Noam Chomsky: When I was growing up in the 1930s and '40s anti-Semitism was rampant. It wasn't like Nazi Germany but it was pretty serious—it was part of life. So, for example, when my father was able to buy a secondhand car in the late 1930s, and he took us to the countryside for a weekend, if we looked for a motel to stay in we had to see if it said "restricted" on it. "Restricted" meant no Jews. You didn't have to say "no blacks," which was something people took for granted. There was also a national policy, which as a child I didn't know anything about. In 1924 the first major immigration law was passed. Before that, there was an Oriental Exclusion Act, but other than that, European immigrants like my parents were generally admitted in the early years of the twentieth century. But that ended in 1924 with an immigration law that was largely directed against Jews and Italians.

JM: Was it connected to the Red Scare?

Chomsky: Well, sort of—in the background. It was right after Woodrow Wilson's first serious post-World War I repression, which deported thousands of people, effectively destroyed unions and independent press, and so on. Right after that, the anti-immigration law was passed that remained in place until the 1960s. And that was the reason why very few people fleeing the rise of fascism in Europe, especially in Germany, could get to the United States. And there were famous incidents like with the *MS Saint Louis*, which brought a lot of immigrants, mostly Jewish, from Europe. It reached Cuba, with people expecting to be admitted to the United States from there. But the administration of Franklin D. Roosevelt wouldn't allow them in and they had to go back to Europe where many of them died in concentration camps.

JM: There were cases involving different countries as well.

Chomsky: It's a lesser-known story, but the Japanese government (after the Russian-Nazi pact, which split Poland) did allow Polish Jews to come to Japan, with the expectation that they would then be sent to the United States. But they weren't accepted, so they stayed in Japan. There's an interesting book called The Fugu Plan, written by Marvin Tokayer and Mary Swartz, which describes the circumstances when European Jews came to Japan, a semi-feudal society.

After World War II there were many Jews who remained in refugee camps…President Harry F. Truman called for the Harrison Commission to investigate the situation in the camps and it was a pretty gloomy report. There were very few Jews admitted into the United States.

JM: These policies had many other lasting consequences.

Chomsky: Of course. The Zionist movement based in Palestine pretty much took over the camps and instituted the policy that every man and woman between the ages of seventeen and thirty-five should be directed to Palestine—not allowed to go to the West. A 1998 study was done in Hebrew by an Israeli scholar, Yosef Grodzinsky, and the English translation of the title is *Good Human Material*. That's what they wanted sent to Palestine for colonization and for the eventual conflict that took place some years later. These policies were somewhat complementary to the U.S. policy of pressuring England to allow Jews to go to Palestine, but not allowing them here. The British politician Ernest Bevin was quite bitter about it, asking, "if you want to save the Jews, why send them to Palestine when you don't admit them?" I suspect most likely that more Nazis came to America. I was a student at Harvard during the early 1950s. There was practically no Jewish faculty there.

JM: According to some articles, Franklin Roosevelt, when he was a member of the board at Harvard, felt there were too many Jews in the college.

Chomsky: There's an interesting book about that called *The Third Reich and the Ivory Tower*, written by Stephen H. Norwood. It has a long discussion about Harvard, and indeed the school's president, James Conant, did block Jewish faculty. He was the one who prevented European Jews from being admitted to the chemistry department—his field—and also had pretty good relations with the Nazis. When Nazi emissaries came to the United States, they were welcomed at Harvard.

JM: It's something that was very common at the time, however today nobody seems willing to accept it.

Chomsky: In general, the attitude towards Nazi Germany was not that hostile, especially if you look at the U.S. State Department reports. In 1937 the State Department was describing Adolf Hitler as a "moderate" who was holding off the forces of the right and the left. In the Munich agreement in late 1938, Roosevelt sent his chief adviser Sumner Welles, who came back with a very supportive statement saying that Hitler was someone we could really do business with and so on. George Kennan is another extreme case. He was the American consul in Berlin until the war between Germany and the United States broke out in December 1941. And until then he was writing pretty supportive statements back stressing that we shouldn't be so hard on the Nazis if they were doing something we didn't agree with—basically repeating the idea that they were people we could do business with. The British had an even stronger business interest in Nazi Germany. And Benito Mussolini was greatly admired.

On racism of every color

JM: In addition to anti-Semitism and racism toward African Americans, there were other groups that suffered. For example, during the 1930s around half a million Mexican Americans were blamed for the Great Depression and deported in various ways. And most of them were U.S. citizens.

Chomsky: Well, there's a strong nativist tradition—saying, "we have to protect ourselves"—that comes from the founding of the country. If you read Benjamin Franklin, who was one of the leading figures of the Enlightenment in the United States and the most distinguished representative of the movement here, he actually advised that the newly founded republic should block Germans and Swedes because they were too "swarthy"—dark.

JM: Why is that pattern of fear historically repeated?

Chomsky: There's a strange myth of Anglo-Saxonism. When the University of Virginia was founded by Thomas Jefferson, for example, its law school offered the study of "Anglo-Saxon Law." And that myth of Anglo-Saxonism carries right over into the early twentieth century. Every wave of immigrants who came were treated pretty badly, but when they all finally became integrated, all of us became Anglo-Saxons.

JM: Like the Irish. They were brutally persecuted, suffered violence because of their orange colored hair and their Catholicism, and then became "assimilated," instead of being "integrated."

Chomsky: The Irish were treated horribly, even here in Boston. For example, in the late nineteenth century they were treated pretty much like African Americans. You could find signs here in Boston in the restaurants saying "No dogs and Irish." Finally they were accepted into society and became part of the political system, and there were Kennedys, and so on. But the same is true about other waves of immigrants, like the Jews in the 1950s. If you take a look at places like Harvard, it's striking. In the early '50s, I think there were a handful of Jewish professors, three or four. But by the 1960s, there were Jewish deans and administrators. In fact, one of the reasons why MIT became a great university was because they admitted Jews whereas Harvard did not.

JM: We can see changes in certain cases, but we can also see things that repeat themselves, such as now in the case of Mexicans and Muslims.

Chomsky: Yes, and Syrians. There is a horrible crisis there and the United States has admitted virtually none of the refugees. The most dramatic case is that of the Central Americans. Why are people fleeing Central America? It's because of the atrocities the U.S. committed there. Take Boston, where there's a fairly large Mayan population. These people are fleeing from the highlands of Guatemala, where there was virtual genocide in the early 1980s backed by Ronald Reagan. The region was devastated, and people are still fleeing to this day, yet they're sent back. Just recently, the administration of Barack Obama, which has broken all sorts of records in regards to deportation, picked up a Guatemalan man living here. I think he had been living here for twenty-five years, had a family, a business, and so on. He had fled from the

Mayan region and they picked him up and deported him. To me, that's really sick.

JM: In the case of Guatemala, the story began in 1954 with the CIA military coup organized against the democratically elected President Jacobo Árbenz.

Chomsky: Yes, it basically began in 1954, and there were other awful atrocities in the late '60s, but the worst happened in the '80s. There was a really monstrous and almost literal genocide in the Mayan area, specifically under Ríos Montt. By now it has been recognized somewhat by Guatemalan society. In fact, Montt was under trial for some crimes. But the U.S. prohibits people from fleeing here. The Obama administration has pressured Mexico to keep them away from the Mexican border, so that they don't succeed in reaching the United States. Pretty much the same thing Europeans have done to Turks and Syrians.

JM: Actually, under international law children should not, in principle, be detained when crossing a non-neighboring country's border. The American Homeland Security Act of 2002 recognizes the same rights. However, this basic law has been broken many times.

Chomsky: A lot of countries break (or go against) the international law… There had been a free and open election in Haiti in the early 1990s and president Jean-Bertrand Aristide won, a populist priest. A few months later came the expected military coup—a very vicious military junta took over, of which the United States was passively supportive. Not openly, of course, but Haitians started to flee from the terror and were sent back and on towards Guantanamo Bay. Of course, that is against International Law. But the United States pretended that they were "economic refugees."

The Spanish Civil War in the basis of Chomsky's thinking

JM: Let's go back very quickly to your contact with the Spanish anarchists. How important was the Spanish Civil War for your social thinking and activism?

Chomsky: Quite important. Actually, my first article—

JM: Which you wrote when you were eleven years old—

Chomsky: Ten, actually. It wasn't about the anarchists; it was about the fall of Barcelona and the spread of fascism over Europe, which was frightening. But a couple of years later I became interested in the anarchist movement.

I had relatives in New York City who I stayed with. And in those days, the area from Union Square down Fourth Avenue had small bookstores, many of which were run by Spanish immigrants who'd fled after Franco's victory. I spent time in them, and also in the offices of Freie Arbeiter Stimme (Free Worker's Voice) with anarchists. I picked up a lot of material and talked to people, and it became a major influence. When I wrote about the Spanish Civil War many years later, I used documents that I picked up when I was a child, as a lot hadn't been published (a lot more resources are available now). I also learned from reading the left-wing press about the Roosevelt administration's indirect support for Francisco Franco, which was not well known, and still isn't.

JM: Apparently Roosevelt regretted that decision but it was too late and the fact is that many other major corporations like ALCOA, GM, and Texaco were crucial for the defeat of the Second Republic—the only democratic experiment in Spain after centuries if we don't consider the almost nonexistent First Republic during the nineteenth century. Many big companies collaborated with the Nazis and Franco.

Chomsky: It was reported in the left-wing press in the late 1930s that the Texas Company (Texaco), headed by the Nazi sympathizer Torkild Rieber, diverted its oil shipments from the Republic, with which it had contracts, to Franco. The State Department denied they knew about it but years later admitted it to be true. You can read it in history books now, but they often suppress the fact that the U.S. government tolerated it. It's really remarkable because they claim that Roosevelt was impeded by the Neutrality Act. On the other hand, he bitterly condemned a Mexican businessman for sending several guns to the Republic. If you look back, oil was the one commodity that Franco could not receive from the Germans and the Italians, so that was quite significant.

JM: All of that sounds familiar.

Chomsky: During the terrorist regime in Haiti in the 1990s, the CIA, under the administration of Bill Clinton, was reporting to Congress that oil shipments had been blocked from entering Haiti. That was just a lie. I was there. You could see the oil terminals being built and the ships coming in. And it turned out that Clinton had authorized Texaco, the same company, to illegally ship oil to the military junta during a time when we were supposedly opposing the military junta and supporting democracy instead.

Same company, same story, but the press wouldn't report it. They must have known. If you look at the Associated Press wires, there's a constant flow of information coming in. At that time I happened to have direct access to AP wires. The day the marines landed in Haiti and restored Aristide there was a lot of excitement about the dedication to democracy and so on. But the day before the marines landed, when every journalist was looking at Haiti because it was assumed that something big was happening, the AP wires reported that the Clinton administration had authorized Texaco to ship oil illegally to the military junta. I wrote an article about the marine landing right away, but barely mentioned the oil, because my article would come out two months later and I assumed by then, "of course, everybody knows." Nobody knew. There was a news report in the Wall Street Journal, in the petroleum journals, and in some small newspapers, but not in the mainstream press. And it was kind of a repeat of what happened in the late ’30s but this was under Clinton, mind you. These are some pretty ugly stories—not ancient history.

JM: Do you think the Spanish anarchists’ experience, had they not been destroyed by Franco, could be used as an example of a third position (to Stalinism, fascism, and Western capitalism)?

Chomsky: Well, the communists were mainly responsible for the destruction of the Spanish anarchists. Not just in Catalonia—the communist armies mainly destroyed the collectives elsewhere. The communists basically acted as the police force of the security system of the Republic and were very much opposed to the anarchists, partially because Stalin still hoped at that time to have some kind of pact with Western countries against Hitler. That, of course, failed and Stalin withdrew the support to the Republic. They even withdrew the Spanish gold reserves.

JM: The fourth largest in the world.

Chomsky: But before that, the anarchist movement was one of their main enemies… There’s an interesting question, whether the anarchists had alternatives. If they did tend to support the government that had been destroyed, what were the alternatives? There was actually a proposal by Camillo Berneri, an Italian anarchist who was in Spain at the time, which is not a crazy notion in my opinion. He opposed participation in government and was against the formation of an army, meaning a major army to fight Franco. He said they should resort to guerrilla war. Which has a history in Spain.

JM: Particularly at the beginning of the nineteenth century under the French occupation.

Chomsky: Under Napoleon Bonaparte's occupation, yes. The same method could have been implemented during the Spanish Civil War, a guerrilla war against Franco's invaders. But Berneri also advocated a political war. Franco's army was mainly Moorish. They were recruiting people from Morocco to come to Spain. There was an uprising in Morocco at the time led by Abd el-Krim (whose tactics influenced Ho Chi Minh and Che Guevara) that sought independence for Morocco and Northern Africa. Berneri proposed that the anarchists should link up with the effort of Northern Africa to overthrow the Spanish government, carry out land reform, attract the base of the Moorish army, and see if they could undermine Franco's army through political warfare in Northern Africa combined with guerrilla warfare in Spain. Historians laughed at that, but I don't think they should have. This was the kind of war that might have succeeded in stopping Spanish fascism.

JM: There were few other successful cases of guerrilla resistance in the world.

Chomsky: There are cases—for example, the American Revolution. George Washington's army lost just about every battle with the British, who had a much better army. The war was basically won by guerrilla forces that managed to undermine the British occupation. The American Revolution was a small part of a major world war going on between France and England, so the

French intervened and that was a big factor, but the domestic contribution was basically guerrilla warfare. George Washington hated the guerrillas. He wanted to imitate the British red coat armies, fighting as gentlemen are supposed to fight. There are very interesting books about these events, for instance one by a very well-known American historian named William R. Polk called *Violent Politics*. It's a record of what are basically guerrilla wars from the American Revolution right up through the wars in Afghanistan and Iraq. He discusses the Spanish guerrilla war against Napoleon and other cases where the conflict turns into a political war, and the invader, who usually has overwhelming power, loses because they can't fight the political war. Against this kind of background, I don't think that the Berneri proposal was that absurd.

Our conversation continued informally on other topics, the most important being human intellectual capability. We touched on language, which has made possible communication, art, and liberation, while at the same time allows for deception and conscious oppression. The most serious current threats to human existence, according to Chomsky, are nuclear weapons and environmental catastrophe.

In my copy of his 1957 book *Syntactic Structures* (considered the most influential book of the twentieth century in the cognitive sciences and among the most important one hundred books ever published), Chomsky wrote for me his legendary sentence:

"Colorless green ideas dream furiously." Grammatically correct but semantically nonsensical, it's the equivalent of $E=mc^2$ for linguistics. Below this he added humorously: "Revolutionary new ideas appear infrequently."

I gave him *Memory of Fire* by my dear friend Eduardo Galeano, who died last year, and Chomsky remembered him with affection. Right or wrong, both men have taught generations to never accept Stockholm syndrome, to never be accomplice to the crimes of arbitrary powers. Both men have taught us that memory and history aren't always the same thing.

(2016)

VIII. In the Manner of Fiction

The Walled Society

With the passing of the years, and thanks to his attentive observation of his clients, Doctor Salvador Uriburu had discovered that the majority of the population of Calataid lacked the European origin of which it boasted. In its eyes, in its hands, persisted the African slaves who repaired the walls in the nineteenth century, and surely the older slaves who built the cisterns in the times of Garama. In its ritual gestures persisted the followers of Kahina, the priestess of the African desert who converted to Judaism before the arrival of Islam. Within the white minority there was also noteworthy diversity, but this had been placed on hold while they were busy considering themselves the representative (and founding) class of the town. The same blue eyes could be found behind Russian eyelids or behind other Irish ones; the same blonde hair could cover a German cranium or another, Gallegan one. How is it possible, Salvador Uriburu had written, that such a diverse town could be so racist and, at the same time, so overflowing with patriotism, with so much fanatical love for one and the same flag? How can the whole be worshiped and at the same time the parts that comprise it disdained? It can't. Unless patriotic reverence is nothing more than the necessary lie nourished by one part in order to use the other parts for its own benefit.

In one of his final public appearances, in May of 1967 in the hall of notables of the Liberty Club, Doctor Uriburu had attempted an exercise that bothered the new traditionalists, once they were able to decipher how it questioned things. Salvador Uriburu had drawn, on a blackboard, a series of at least fifteen triangles, circles and squares. When he asked those present how many kinds of drawings they saw there, everyone agreed that they saw three. When he asked that they select one of those three types, everyone chose the group of triangles and the doctor asked them again how many groups they saw in the group of triangles. Everyone said that there were at least two groups: a group of isosceles triangles and a group of right triangles.

"More or less isosceles and more or less right-angled" said one discerningly, noticing that the drawings were not perfect.

"The figures aren't perfect," confirmed Salvador Uriburu, "just like human beings. And like human beings everyone saw first the differences, those that made the figures different, before seeing what they had in common."

"That's not true," said someone, "the triangles have something in common among themselves. Each one has three sides, three angles."

"The circles and the squares also have something in common: they are all geometrical figures. But nobody observed that there was also one unique group of drawings, the group of geometrical figures."

Salvador Uriburu neither made accusations nor clarified the example, as was his custom. But after months of arguing about the strange and pedantic exposition of the doctor's little figures, the pastor George Ruth Guerrero arrived at the conclusion that this kind of thinking came to the little doctor from the sect of humanists and, most certainly, the Illuminati.

"The group of geometrical figures," concluded the pastor with his index finger in the air, "represented humanity and each group of figures represented a race, a religion, a deviation and so on and so forth. The humanists would like to make us believe that the truth does not exist; that the faith of the Moors and of the Jews is the same as the true faith of the Christians, the race of the chosen ones and the race of the sinners, the morality of our fathers and the sodomy of the moderns, the garments of our women and the indecent nudity of the Nigerians."

They accused the doctor of being a gnostic. It was known, by rumors and magazines from France, that the Heterodox one had conquered the rest of Europe with an extraordinary belief: the truth did not exist; any heresy could be taken as a substitute for the true faith and logical reason. And it was said that someone was trying to introduce all of that in Calataid.

The allusion was direct, but Doctor Uriburu did not respond. The last time he entered the hall of notables, in August of 1967, it was expected that he would say that he was for or against this superstition, that he would define, once and for all, which side he was on. Instead, he came out with another of his figures that had nothing to do with his profession as a scientist, much less as a believer, which demonstrated his irremediable descent into mysticism, into the sect of the Illuminati who, it was said, assembled every Thursday in an unknown chamber of the old cisterns.

"Once there was a man who climbed a mountain of sand," he said, "and upon arriving at the peak he decided it was the only mountain in the desert. Nevertheless, right away he realized that others had done the same, from other peaks. Then he said that his mountain, the one beneath his feet, was the true one. Then the man, or perhaps it was a woman, decided to come down from his dune and he climbed another one and then another, until he understood (perhaps from atop the highest dune) that there were many dunes, an infinite number relative to his strength. Then, tired, he said that the desert was not one sand dune in particular, but all of the dunes together. He said that there were some tall dunes and other smaller ones, and that just one fistful of sand from any of them didn't represent one dune in particular but the entire desert, and that nobody, like none of the dunes, was the desert, completely. He also said that the dunes moved, that the true dune which allowed the unique perspective of the desert and of itself changed again and again in size and place, and that to ignore that was to deny an inseparable part of any unique truth.

"Unlike some other exhausted traveler, this discovery did not lead him to deny the existence of all of the dunes, only the arbitrary pretense that there was just one in the immensity of the desert. He denied that a handful of sand had less value and less permanence than that arbitrary and pretentious dune. That is to say, he denied some ideas and affirmed others; he was not indifferent to the eternal search for truth. And for that very reason he was persecuted in the name of the desert, until a sand storm put an end to the dispute."

An indescribable silence followed the doctor's new enigma. Then a repressed murmur filled the hall. Someone stood to announce the end of the meeting and reminded everyone of the date of the next one. The bell sounded; everyone rose and left without acknowledging him. He knew that they were also bothered that he would doubt the tolerance and freedom of Calataid, making use of metaphors as if he were a victim of the inquisition or living in the times of the barbarous Nero.

Uriburu remained seated, watching through the window the old men and young lads who rode by on their bicycles and could not see him, with his hands in the pockets of his suit coat, playing with a handful of sand. He lost his mind twenty days later. A strange diagnosis, written in his own hand, concluded that Calataid suffered from "social autism." Autism, according to the books, is a product of the accelerated growth of the brain that, instead of increasing intelligence reduces it or renders it useless due to the pressure of the encephalic mass against the walls of the craneum. For Doctor Uriburu, who was more concerned with architecture than with biology, the walls of Calataid had provoked the same effect with the growth in the population's pride. Therefore, it was useless to pretend to cure individuals if the society was sick. In fact, to suppose that society and individuals are two different things is an artifice of the view and of the medicine that identifies bodies, not spirits. And Calataid was incapable of relating two different facts with a common explanation. Even more: it was incapable of recognizing its own memory, engraved scandalously on the stones, in the dank voids of its interiors, and denied or covered over by the most recent invention of a tradition.

(2004)

The Age of Barbaria

Annual trips back to the year 33 began in the Age of Barbaria. That year was selected because, according to surveys, Christ's crucifixion drew the attention of most Westerners, and this social sector was important for economic reasons since trips to the past weren't organized, much less financed, by the government of any country (as had once happened with the first trips into space) but by a private company. The financial group that made the marvel of traveling through time possible was called Axa. Acting at the request of the High Chief of Technology, who suggested infinite profits through "tourism services," Axa transported groups of thirty people each to the year 33 in order to witness the death of the Nazarene, much as the tourist commoners did long ago when at each equinox they would gather at the foot of the pyramid of Chitchen-Itzá to witness the formation of the serpent from the shadows cast down by the pyramid upon itself.

The greatest inconvenience encountered by Axa was the limited number of tourists who were able to attend the event at one time, thus hampering the millions in profit expected by the investors. For this reason, the group maximum was gradually raised to forty-five, at the risk of attracting the attention of the ancient residents of Jerusalem. That figure has been maintained at the request of one of the company's principal stockholders, who argued, reasonably, that the conservation of that historic deed in its original state was the basis for the trips, and that if each group produced alterations to the facts, it could result in an abandonment of general interest in carrying out this kind of travel.

Over time it has been proven that each historical alteration of the facts, no matter how small, is nearly impossible to repair. Such damage occurs whenever one of the travelers fails to respect the rules and attempts to take away some memento of the place. The most well-known was the case of Adam Parker who, with incredible dexterity, was able to cut out a triangular piece of the Nazarene's red tunic, probably at the moment the latter collapsed from fatigue. The theft did not signify any change in the holy scriptures, but it served to make Parker rich and famous, since the tiny piece of canvas came to be worth a fortune, and more than a few of the travelers who have since taken on the trouble and expense of going back thousands of years have done so to see where the Nazarene is missing "Parker's Triangle."

A few have posed objections to this kind of travel, which, they insist, will end up destroying history in ways beyond our notice. In effect, it has: for each change introduced on any given day, infinite changes are derived from it, century after century, gradually diluting or multiplying its effects. In order to notice a minimal change in the year 33 it would be useless to turn to the

Holy Scriptures, because all of the editions, equally, would reflect the blow and completely forget the original facts. There might be a possibility of tracing each change by projecting other trips to years just prior to the Age of Barbaria, but nobody would be interested in such a project and there would be no way of financing it.

The discussion about whether history should remain as it is or can be legitimately modified also no longer matters. But the latter is, in any case, dangerous, since it is impossible to foresee the resulting changes that would be produced by any particular alteration. We know that any change might not be catastrophic for the human species, but could potentially be catastrophic for individuals: we might not be the ones who are alive now, but someone else instead.

The most radical religious groups find themselves on opposing sides. Barbaria's information services have recently discovered that a group of Evangelicals belonging to the True Church of God in Sao Pablo, will make a trip to the year 33. Thanks to the charity of its faithful, the group has managed to gather together the sum of several million charged by Axa per ticket. What no one has yet been able to confirm are the group's intentions. It's been said they will blow up Golgotha and set fire to Jerusalem at the moment of the Crucifixion, so that we thus arrive at the greatly anticipated End Times. All of history would disappear; the whole world, including the Jews, would recognize their error and would turn to Christianity in the year 33. The entire world would live in the Kingdom of God, just as described in the Gospels.

Others dispute this as conspiracy theory, or they question how the travelers could witness the Crucifixion without trying to prevent it. The theological answer is obvious, which is why those least interested in preventing the martyrdom of the Messiah are his own followers. But for the rest, who are the majority, Axa has decreed its own ethical rules: "In the same manner in which we do not prevent the death of the slave between the claws of a lion when we travel to Africa, neither must we prevent the apparent injustices that are committed with the Nazarene. Our moral duty is to conserve nature and history as they are." The crucifixion is the common heritage of humanity, but, above all, its rights have been acquired totally by Axa.

In fact, the changes will be increasingly inevitable. After six years of trips to the year 33, one can see, at the foot of the cross, bottle caps and magic marker graffiti on the main beam, some of which pray: "I have faith in my lord," and others just limit themselves to the name of who was there, along with the date of departure, so that future generations of travelers will remember them. Of course, the company also began to yield in the face of pressure from dissatisfied clients, leading to a radical improvement in services. For example, Barbaria just sent a technical representative to the year 26 to request the production of five thousand cubic meters of asphalt and to negotiate with Pontius Pilate the construction of a more comfortable corridor for the Via

Dolorosa, which will make less tiresome the travelers' route and, besides, would be a gesture of compassion for the Nazarene, who more than once broke his feet on stones that he failed to see in his path. It has been calculated that the improvement won't mean changes in the Holy Scriptures, since there is no special concern demonstrated there for the urbanism of the city.

With these measures, Axa hopes to shelter itself from the storm of complaints it has received due to alleged inadequacies in service, having to confront recently very costly lawsuits brought by clients who have spent a fortune and have returned unsatisfied. The cause of these complaints is not always the intense heat of Jerusalem, or the congestion in which the city is entrapped on the day of the Crucifixion. Above all the cause is the unsatisfied expectations of the travelers. The company defends itself by saying that the Holy Scriptures weren't written under its quality control, but instead are only historical documents and, therefore, are exaggerated. There where the Nazarene really dies, instead of a deep and horrifying night, the sky is barely darkened by an excessive concentration of clouds, and nothing more. The Catholics have declared that this fact, like all those referenced in the Gospels, should be understood in its symbolic meaning and not merely descriptively. But most people were satisfied neither by Axa's response nor by that of Pope John XXV, who came out in defense of the multinational corporation, thanks to which people can now be closer to God.

(2005)

In the Land of the Free and the Brave

Several people in the asylum, maybe five or six, surrounded us with their wooden guns in order to pay homage to the heroes. One of them (a man with very short hair that shone like fire in the darkness above a little cross tattooed at the nape of his neck) said that his gun was symbolic of freedom and he had reason to own one. It because he was free to defend himself and he felt comfortable enough with the feel of it stuck in his belt.

That feeling of freedom was growing over time, whereby he could no longer sleep if he didn't have his gun underneath the pillow. And because he was living in a free country and was carrying (loading?) a gun, and the country was free because others were carrying (loading?) their guns.

But, since he couldn't fly with weapons, he didn't fly. And since he couldn't go around with weapons in other countries, he didn't travel outside of his own. He lived in the land of the free and the brave, but he wasn't brave enough to be able to live without his gun nor was he free enough to know the rest of the world (in other words, almost the whole world) where the people roam the streets with only their fists.

(2010)

INDEX

C

V

W

X

Z

Notes

www.ingramcontent.com/pod-product-compliance
Lightning Source LLC
LaVergne TN
LVHW011216080426
835509LV00005B/147

* 9 7 8 1 7 3 3 2 0 8 1 1 6 *